SATRAPS, COALITIONS AND POWER GAMES

SATRAPS, COALITIONS AND POWER GAMES

SUNITA ARON

Vitasta

Published by
Renu Kaul Verma
Vitasta Publishing Pvt Ltd
4348/4C, Ansari Road, Daryaganj
New Delhi - 110 002
info@vitastapublishing.com

ISBN: 978-81-19670-15-4

First Edition 2025
MRP 595

Edited by Oswald Pereira
Layout by Shubhpreet Kaur
Cover Design by Rohit Gautam
Printed by Chaman Enterprises, New Delhi

To the voters of India who belie the belief that only the literate have political wisdom.

Contents

Preface

Power comes from numbers in a parliamentary democracy, whether there are two poles or three poles around which the politics of the country revolves. And, when invincibility of national parties declines, the inevitability of regional parties grows.

Big, small or tiny, regional parties are transforming the electoral politics of the country.

Some political scientists dub them as destabilising forces without any well-defined ideological position, but despite their rusticity, their supporters applaud them for seeing the opportunity in a scenario of weakening national parties.

Politics is a ruthless game of power play. Regional parties, which come in various shapes and sizes, so very cleverly follow the dictum: *hum power ke liye kuch bhi karenge* (we will do anything for power).

As a political commentator, watching the country's ever-changing politics and the accompanying power games has been interesting, even exciting and entertaining. A classic example of this bizarre yet exciting politics is the case of the volatile state of Uttar Pradesh, which gave the country a 48-hour Loktantrik

Congress Party chief minister Jagdambika Pal (now in the BJP). It was such high-octane drama for two days.

Little wonder then some journalists have described the manoeuvrings of politicians and their parties as India's new electoral box offices.

As regional parties rule the roost, calling the shots in government formation and policies, there's been a cry for a return to the two-party system.

But then the question arises: Wouldn't a two-party system limit the multiple choices that the voters have today? As politics of the two national parties, the Bharatiya Janata Party (BJP) and the Congress, increasingly gets centralised with regional satraps either disappearing or falling silent, these small outfits offer hope by becoming the voice of the people living in far-flung regions.

Moreover, while voters may find 'Delhi far and Lucknow close,' say in UP, the fact remains that the national parties are equally dependent on regional parties to meet their political aspirations, notwithstanding power sharing.

Om Prakash Rajbhar, president of the tiny Suheldev Bharatiya Samaj Party (SBSP), shook hands with Union home minister Amit Shah in Delhi and ensured his re-entry into Yogi 2.0, despite the unpalatable words he had fired at Adityanath. Rajbhar, in return, agreed to support the BJP in the 2024 General Elections. Soon after becoming cabinet minister in UP, the irrepressible Rajbhar told his supporters at a public rally to 'wear a *peela gamchcha* (yellow muffler) and barge into any police station and announce that I have sent you. The DM, SP and CO have no powers to call and confirm from me.'

Rajbhar had founded the SBSP in 2002. It is a registered party, but remains unrecognised. Its area of influence includes some pockets of East UP, but Rajbhar is courted even by a big party like the BJP, because in electoral battles, every vote and every seat matters.

Again, in Maharashtra, we saw a thriller recently as regional parties broke ranks for power or protection from investigating agencies. The 'home-breakers' were promised power as they had laid the foundation for a BJP government in the state. In the give and take, former BJP chief minister Devendra Fadnavis became Deputy CM to Eknath Shinde, who was rewarded for breaking his political home, the Shiv Sena. This showed, all is fair in love and war. Ethics in politics is only meant for academic discussions.

Once, when Samajwadi Party founder president Mulayam Singh Yadav was asked about his power politics of ambivalence, he had rebutted with, 'We are in politics to attain power and not play drums.'

To put it succinctly and bluntly, the game of thrones is unscrupulously played by all.

Indeed, the political history of the country is full of histrionics that proves the power and prowess of regional parties. In this context, two interesting examples come to mind. The examples are the fall of the Atal Bihari Vajpayee government in 1999 and the clearance of the landmark Indo-US nuclear deal in 2008.

The country's then most popular leader Vajpayee had formed a coalition government in 1998. Barely thirteen months later, he had to face a no-confidence motion after the BJP's coalition partner, J Jayalalithaa, president of the All India Anna Dravida Munnetra Kazhagam (AIADMK), withdrew support to his government. He lost the numerical battle by just one vote, as against the NDA's 269 votes, the Opposition secured 270.

The silent Prime Minister Manmohan Singh, whose actions always spoke more than his words, had signed a landmark Indo-US nuclear deal in 2005, amidst fierce protest from the

Communists, who were supporting his minority government from outside. Singh had refused to budge under pressure, boldly telling Communist leaders, 'If you want to withdraw support, so be it.' Mulayam Singh Yadav of the Samajwadi Party, with thirty-nine members in the Lok Sabha, had bailed out the tottering UPA government by supporting the Indo-US nuclear deal in the Lok Sabha in 2008. Mulayam always described it as his career's best decision.

'We had met the former president APJ Abdul Kalam who explained how the deal was in the nation's interest and would not compromise the nation's sovereignty,' he said later. However, not always have political parties acted in national interest.

In a large country like India with diverse cultures, regional parties started growing since 1967, two decades after the country attained Independence. For the first time, they captured the throne in 1977 and then again in 1989. In this decade-long period, they mushroomed and grew illogically ambitious after Janata Dal leader HD Deve Gowda with forty-six MPs became Prime Minister. It took the national parties almost a decade to tackle them and form the National Democratic Alliance (NDA) and the United Progressive Alliance (UPA). Stability replaced perfidy.

Interestingly, even after the BJP's spectacular victory in the 2014 and 2019 polls, the coalition era has continued as Narendra Modi did not demolish the NDA and gave representation to its members in his government. It paid him dividends in 2024, when he fell short of numbers.

Telugu Desam Party leader N Chandrababu Naidu had brilliantly summed up the sentiments of the regional parties, which represent regional aspirations. After congratulating Prime Minister Narendra Modi on 7 June 2024, Naidu said, 'Balancing regional aspirations and national interests must run parallelly, while ensuring holistic development for all strata of society.'

Between 1989 and 2014 when BJP won a majority, India had witnessed seven consecutive elections in which no single party was able to achieve the magical majority. Obviously, the minority governments gave ample space to the regional parties for bargaining and blackmail in the absence of any provisions in the rule book to check opportunistic alliances.

Many political scientists connect the growth of regional parties to the weakening of Congress, dubbed the grand old party, as it suffered several splits and its splinter groups spread across the country giving rise to regional parties. Thereafter, the Janata Dal, a conglomeration of several non-Congress parties, broke and its branches opened in different states. Ironically, the rise of the mighty BJP also failed to check their proliferation.

Instead, when the most powerful Prime Minister Narendra Modi needed numerical strength in the Lok Sabha for a third consecutive term in 2024, two of his estranged partners—Telugu Desam Party (TDP) and the Janata Dal (U)—offered support.

History was repeating itself. Coalition dharma was again embraced with a smile.

Interestingly, Shiv Sena (Shinde) and NCP (Ajit Pawar) brought seven and one Lok Sabha seats, respectively, to the NDA kitty.

It was a well-planned manoeuvre. The BJP high command had engineered defections in the Shiv Sena and the NCP ahead of the 2024 Lok Sabha elections. Two more regional parties were added in the state, which had largely remained bi-polar till Maratha leader Sharad Pawar broke the Congress in 1978.

The numbers, which play a critical role in parliamentary democracy, also tell us about the relevance of regional parties in the country. That is the fact of the matter.

In the 18th Lok Sabha, the two major national parties, the BJP and the Congress, accounted for 240 and ninety-nine seats, respectively. Of the other four national parties, the BSP and the NPP failed to open their accounts, while CPI(M) and Aam Aadmi Party won four and three seats respectively.

The Samajwadi Party, a regional party in Uttar Pradesh, emerged as the third largest party winning thirty-seven seats. In all, forty-one big and small regional parties, have their representation in the Lok Sabha.

In 2019, thirty-six parties were represented in the Lok Sabha, when the national party, namely the BJP, had performed its best, picking 346 seats.

Of the thirty chief ministers of states and Union territories, the regional parties head governments in thirteen of them independently or in alliance with a national party.

The BJP dominates the political landscape ruling fourteen states (after Manipur went under President's rule), but has yet to crack the prominent states of the South—Tamil Nadu and Andhra Pradesh, Telangana and Kerala—as well as West Bengal, Bihar, Punjab, Jammu and Kashmir, to name a few. The Congress has been relegated to three states only.

Ironically, before saffron started sweeping the country since 2014, the BJP was humming the *Congress Mukt Bharat* tune. But they soon realised the real challenge came from the regional parties, as they thwarted their plans to build a pan-India presence.

This book is an effort to answer the question why and how regional parties mushroom, why they patronise families and why they will remain relevant for times to come. It's more of a narration with some samples and stories to answer the big Why?

A special mention has been made about Shiromani Akali Dal,

the oldest party in the country, the Aam Aadmi Party (AAP), a new political phenomenon, the Bahujan Samaj Party (BSP), which became the voice of Dalits, and the Jharkhand Mukti Morcha (JMM) representing tribal aspirations.

Now, as regional parties grow old and their founder-members ail or age, a new crop of young leadership has emerged on the political horizon, including Akhilesh Yadav in UP, Tejashwi Yadav in Bihar, Udhayanidhi Stalin in Tamil Nadu and Nara Lokesh in Andhra Pradesh. Their challenges are huge even if they have inherited or will inherit robust political parties, for along with the inheritance comes a huge baggage in the form of image of the party and idiosyncrasies of their leaders. They have started reinventing themselves at a time when the politics of the country is changing, with investigations and incarcerations becoming the order of the day.

There will be defections or divisions, but the regional parties are also learning to hold onto their turf and survive.

Chapter 1

The Rise of Regional Powerhouses

Socialist leader and founding member of the Samajwadi Party (SP), Beni Prasad Verma, an all-weather friend of three-time UP Chief Minister Mulayam Singh Yadav, had an embarrassing moment when he was caught red-handed after his clandestine meeting with Kanshi Ram, the Bahujan Samaj Party (BSP) founder President.

The incident dates back to the early 1990s when the Samajwadi Party had formed a coalition government with the BSP in which Verma was a cabinet minister, second only in rank to CM Mulayam Singh Yadav. The government had not even completed a year when it started tottering due to acute differences between the coalition partners.

Kanshi Ram started plotting a change in leadership as his protégé Mayawati was eyeing the chief ministership. The BSP was a junior partner with sixty-seven MLAs against the SP's 109. The Congress had extended outside support to the coalition government in its bid to stall the Bharatiya Janata Party (BJP) from forming the government.

Significantly, the BJP was the single largest party with 177

MLAs, thirty-six short of the majority mark in a house of 425 members in the then undivided Uttar Pradesh but an unfriendly Governor in Raj Bhawan refused to entertain its claim to form the government.

Kanshi Ram decided to snap ties with the SP, emboldened by the willingness of the Congress to join hands with him in toppling the government. He contacted Beni Prasad Verma, offering him the CM's post on the condition that he divide his fledgling party.

Mulayam Singh Yadav had formed the SP in October 1992 after his frustrating stints in several Socialist parties, including Lok Dal, Lok Dal(B), Janata Party, Samajwadi Janata Party, Krantikari Morcha and Janata Dal.

Importantly, despite being in and out of power, SP continues to dominate the politics of Uttar Pradesh even thirty-two years later.

As an old time socialist, Beni shared Mulayam's angst against political isolation after the demolition of the Babri Mosque in Ayodhya on 6 December 1992. But somewhere in the corner of his heart, Beni had nursed an ambition to be UP CM someday.

Lured by Kanshi Ram's offer of the CM's chair, Beni drove down to his secret meeting with the BSP supremo, accompanied by his most trusted security guard, leaving behind the pilot car to ensure his location was not tracked.

He himself told me later that he was shocked when the wireless set of his trusted security guard buzzed, while he was entering his car to return home after meeting Kanshi Ram.

The caller was Mulayam, asking him about his parleys with the BSP chief.

The SP-BSP government had a traumatic collapse a few days after the 'secret' meeting. It was engineered by the BJP as its leadership was desperate to break the formidable caste coalition under the SP-BSP banner.

Mayawati became CM, shattering Beni's aspiration for the top post. Formed by Kanshi Ram in April 1984 to empower Dalits, the BSP flourished as a regional party after it came to power. Despite its decline over the years, the BSP remains politically relevant today. Both the regional parties, the SP and BSP, have dictated state politics from 1993 to 2017, while the national parties were floundering.

Kanshi Ram often admitted brazenly that lame governments (referring to minority governments) suited them most.

In real politics, hung houses suit regional parties, both new and old, as they get room to dominate and dictate coalition governments.

It is in this scenario that the second phase of the coalition era in the country as well as Uttar Pradesh unfolded in 1989 and lasted till 1999. In UP it ended in 2007. In between, the state was ruled by ten chief ministers besides three spells of President's rule.

During this phase, six governments were formed by political stalwarts at the Centre, but none could complete its five-year term, as the regional parties demanding their share of the cake played spoiler.

The formation of the BJP-led National Democratic Alliance and Congress-led United Progressive Alliance eventually brought stability at the Centre, as a majority of the regional parties found a big brother and berth in government at the national level. UP started voting for majority governments after end of a fourteen-year coalition jinx by the BSP in 2007. During the period, elections had thrown hung houses, leaving room for ambitious political parties to form governments, albeit fragile.

Uttar Pradesh, the country's largest state with eighty Lok

Sabha seats, has always been politically volatile, demanding utmost caution and vigil by CMs of both minority and majority governments.

Mulayam Singh Yadav was not the only CM who kept a constant watch on his ministers, including the trusted ones. Prior to him, Congress CM Vir Bahadur Singh used to hold late night free flow sessions to know what was cooking in his rival group led by Kamlapati Tripathi, a party stalwart from East UP. Even the current CM Yogi Adityanath maintains close surveillance on both truant and the trusted ministers to stay safe in the chair.

As politics increasingly became competitive and unstable, the CMs increased their vigil on both their political friends and foes, which has become easier now in a technological age. Earlier, the leaders had to rely on their informal spies, the party workers, babus and the common people, including peons and file handlers.

Maharashtra is the second-largest state with forty-eight Lok Sabha seats and has been comparatively more stable because of bi-polar politics for many years.

The state saw the birth of two new regional parties in 2022, much to the amusement of the public and agony of their original founders—the latest example of how regional parties are born in the country. To understand this development, it is important to know the background.

Since the country's Independence in 1947 till 1995, the politics of the country's richest state Maharashtra was largely dominated by the Congress, barring a short stint of the Opposition in the post-Emergency period from 1977-1980 when Sharad Pawar had split the Congress and formed a Progressive Democratic Front with the Janata Party. He had become the youngest Chief Minister at the age of 38 and continued in office till February 1980. Forty-five years later, he had a bitter taste of his own recipe.

The second coalition government was formed by Shiv Sena-BJP in 1995. It was replaced by another coalition government of the Congress and its breakaway faction, the Nationalist Congress Party (NCP) in 1999, which ruled the state till 2014. Two ideologically compatible formations surfaced on the state's political horizon with the two big national parties joining hands with a regional force—Congress with NCP and BJP allied with the Shiv Sena.

In 2014, the ambitious BJP and suspicious Shiv Sena snapped their two-decade old alliance over sharing of seats and contested assembly polls independently. The BJP won the battle and formed the government for the next five years from 2014-2019 under the leadership of Devendra Fadnavis.

The beleaguered Shiv Sena, formed by Bal Thackeray in 1966, again joined hands with the BJP for the 2019 Assembly elections and the two together won the numerical majority, only to fall apart a few days later. This time the tussle was over the coveted chair of the Chief Minister.

BJP's Devendra Fadnavis became CM for five days, but resigned before the floor test, as by then, the Shiv Sena had managed to secure the support of its political and ideological rivals—the Congress and its breakaway faction, the NCP—and formed the Maha Vikas Aghadi (MVA), which also formed the government.

The BJP avenged its humiliation by toppling the government after two years and 214 days. It ruthlessly splintered not just the Shiv Sena, but also the NCP to engineer a government collapse.

Thus, there was every reason for CM Uddhav Thackeray and his team to remain vigilant knowing the BJP would be baying for blood. The BJP leadership had not only felt betrayed, but were desperate to win the second most important state in the Lok Sabha elections in May 2024 as well as State Assembly elections in October-November 2024. Political observers say, winning elections while ruling the state is increasingly becoming easier.

Strangely, Uddhav did not learn from his father's blue book. Like Nero, he played the fiddle while his government was on fire.

Shiv Sainiks knew Bal Thackeray never tolerated infidelity, but his son was not a patch on him.

> Those who wanted to break away succeeded if their exits went unnoticed by Thackeray or any of the violent elements in the organisation. But if Thackeray had noticed any of these Shiv Sainiks, then it was well-neigh impossible to disappear quietly. They had to stay put or pay for their desertions, usually with their lives as they had no freedom of Choice. (Sujata Anandan, *Samrat*, page 22, Harper Collins)

In her book, Sujata Anandan has described how Chhagan Bhujbal, a former mayor, could quit the party in 1991 and still lived to tell the tale. 'He joined the then ruling Congress amidst much fear, intimidation and threats. The government had to stretch its resources to the limits and resort to much intrigue to keep Bhujbal alive and protected,' writes Anandan on page 23 of her book, *Samrat.*

While Mulayam Singh Yadav and Bal Thackeray could keep an eye on probable troublemakers in the 1990s, two decades later in 2022, when technology was more advanced and could be used to keep hawk eyes on the movements of every individual, Uddhav Thackeray remained in the dark and failed to nip in the bud the growing rebellion right under his nose, until the government collapsed. The developments did not take place overnight, as many of his loyalists in the Shiv Sena would like to believe.

Political observers said that Uddhav had an inkling about the secret moves, but he wasn't aware of how many Shiv Sainiks were in the rebel camp. By the time he realised the true numbers, it was too late, apparently leaving him with no option but to let them go. His son Aditya Thackeray shared with his confidantes his father's decision of not stopping them, as he knew the 'obliged rebels' would in any way cross over during the floor test.

On the face of it, rebel leader Eknath Shinde, an old Shiv Sainik, was keen to rebuild an alliance with the Sena's natural ally, the BJP. He had repeatedly shared with Uddhav Thackeray his reservations about the party's alliance with the Congress and the NCP, but the Shiv Sena leader did not deem it important to put him under a scanner to track his movements till the disappearing act happened. Shinde was removed from the post of Legislature Party leader, only after the rebellion had flared up.

The political thriller started on the day of the Maharashtra Legislative Council elections for ten seats in the State Assembly on 20 June 2022 and ended on 30 June 2022, after Eknath Shinde usurped power to become the twentieth Chief Minister of Maharashtra with MLAs being the voters.

The forty-odd MLAs, with dreams of becoming ministers in the new Eknath Shinde government or securing a clean chit from criminal and corruption charges from an obliging Central Government, coolly slipped from the State Assembly after crossvoting in the MLC election. By the time the government woke up from its slumber and hurriedly summoned a meeting of lawmakers, Shinde, along with the rebels had left for Surat in Gujarat.

No one was keeping an eye on their movement and location, though the government could have stopped the rebels while they were within Maharashtra. Calls were made but phones were not reachable. Obviously, the phones had been switched off. People were rushed to the homes of the rebels, to their possible hideouts, but it proved to be a futile exercise.

Where were the Intelligence sleuths who kept their CM in the dark? Threats followed, but the rebels were hardly frightened of Uddhav Thackeray, as he was not a terror like his father.

They were comfortably camping in Surat in Gujarat, barely 280 kms from Mumbai. No other city could have been safer than Surat in Prime Minister Narendra Modi's home state of Gujarat for a coup orchestrated by the BJP. Some were on their way, hiding in a hotel in Mumbai when they were caught.

The world witnessed the drama as the rebels ecstatically welcomed every addition to their gang, as MLAs in droves started deserting the Shiv Sena, the sinking ship.

It was no secret that they were laying the foundation of a new regional party—nothing new in India's brazen game of opportunistic politics, where victory goes to the highest bidder.

It was a well-planned and perfectly executed game done with flawless precision. A friendly Governor Bhagat Singh Koshyari was present in the Raj Bhavan to lend a helping hand to the rebels.

Keeping up a charade of fairness, Koshyari invited Uddhav Thackeray for a floor test, but he understandably shied away. Failing to get a stay from the Supreme Court on the floor test, Uddhav had no option but to resign as he knew he lacked the requisite strength to stay on. Next day, on 30 June 2022, a jubilant Shinde took the oath of office and secrecy as CM.

The game was over for the time being as the apex court too failed to give any relief to the outgoing CM, who had stepped down from office. Quite interestingly, the split in the Shiv Sena party was still not official.

Cross petitions were filed by both the factions in the court of the new Assembly Speaker Rahul Narwekar. He announced his verdict in January 2024, declaring the splinter group of Shiv

Sena led by Eknath Shinde as the real Shiv Sena, as it had the support of a majority of the party MLAs.

The former five-day CM Devendra Fadnavis gave a quirky smile and said he had finally avenged his humiliation of 2019. He was often mocked for his poll punchline, 'I will be back.'

After the NCP split in July 2023, he said, 'I have returned to power two and a half years later after splitting both the political parties—Shiv Sena and NCP.' He took pride in splitting the parties and the formation of splinter groups, but paid a heavy price. Because it was BJP that returned to power, and not Fadnavis.

Fadnavis became deputy CM in the Shinde-led government, a demotion from being chief minister in a previous tenure. It was a post he was reluctant to hold, but as BJP's 'disciplined soldier,' he lacked the guts to say no, or perhaps was arm-twisted to accept the diktats of the high command.

Prime Minister Narendra Modi publicly ridiculed Thackeray saying, 'If he can't handle his party, how could he have handled the government.'

Gone were the days of Sena tiger Bal Thackeray when no one could have dared to deceive him and survive too, both in politics or otherwise.

Such was senior Thackeray's confidence in his own leadership that he had officially registered Shiv Sena in 1976, a decade after its formation, as he never foresaw any challenge to the 'Tiger' till then. It was perhaps the fear of the emergency in 1976 that forced him to declare the party hierarchy.

Senior Thackeray had wielded immense power but he also nurtured the party as a family, demanding that Shiv Sainiks support each other in their joys and sorrows. Earlier, when Chhagan Bhujbal had quit the party with seventeen MLAs in the early 1990s, the Sainiks had stood behind the party leadership and vowed to teach the rebels a lesson. But Bal Thackeray's son Uddhav lacked his father's tough traits.

Shinde had grown in the same famous family culture of Shiv Sena which he joined in 1980. He became *Shakha Pramukh* of Thane in 1984. However, he also violated party ethics and rebelled against his high command, as he knew Uddhav lacked his father's stature.

Uddhav is often described as a true gentleman, who wanted to change the character of the party from militant to moderate, but that took him nowhere. When the split happened, neither did Shiv Sainiks burn Mumbai, nor the rebels feared any threat to their lives or political future.

When Uddhav Thackeray's cousin Raj Thackeray had left the party along with several lawmakers and workers in 2006, he had failed to even dent the party, less divide it. Bal Thackeray was then alive and though ailing, he had done much of the damage control. The 'tiger' died in November 2012.

This time, when Shinde took away forty lawmakers, Uddhav, the son of the Sena tiger, remained a mute spectator, and did not react fiercely and forcefully as his father would have responded to the crisis.

The three-party MVA coalition government, of which two were powerful regional parties, silently saw and sat through its demolition, as they either had no strategy to turn the tables on the perpetrators or they gave in before the might of BJP's central leadership.

Shiv Sainiks were shocked as they watched the tragic disintegration of their Tiger's Shiv Sena.

Ostensibly, there was no ideological clash between the BJP and the Shiv Sena as Hindutva was their common plank. It was largely a territorial clash between a regional player and a national party, after the BJP high command violated an informal agreement worked out between their late leader Pramod Mahajan and Bal Thackeray over their area of operations.

Shiv Sena had limited its territorial presence to Maharashtra, while an ambitious BJP high command wanted to spread its wings across the country, including the richest state.

In the early 1990s, Bal Thackeray had sent a contingent of Shiv Sainiks for Kar Seva to liberate the Ayodhya shrine in Uttar Pradesh, though it was purely a Sangh Parivar movement. Thackeray had even monitored the developments in the religiously surcharged temple city on a daily basis, but himself kept away from the limelight and from UP.

This was not the first time when a CM was caught napping and was unseated by tiny regional parties.

The Kalyan Singh government was toppled during the 1998 Lok Sabha elections with the help of smaller, rather inconsequential allies, but deft handling by the BJP leadership and Kalyan Singh himself, got him the chair back within 48 hours after dismantling the minority government installed by a friendly Governor in Raj Bhavan, Romesh Bhandari.

Kalyan Singh had simultaneously fought at various levels—he first managed the law makers of the BJP as well as the supporting parties including the smaller allies; he petitioned the governor and the speaker while his senior minister rushed to the Allahabad High Court and filed a Special Leave Petition and demanded an urgent hearing.

Led by the party's Prime Ministerial candidate Atal Bihari Vajpayee, an indefinite dharna was staged in Delhi after handing over a memorandum to the President.

A multi-pronged strategy was laid out through a flurry of activities in Lucknow, Allahabad and New Delhi which paved the way for Kalyan Singh's reinstatement on the CM's chair. The drama had ended with the country's first ever composite floor test in the State Assembly, which Kalyan won. Jagdambika Pal became the 48-hour CM.

Earlier in 1997, the same Kalyan Singh had divided the Congress and the BSP to win a trust vote after Mayawati had withdrawn support from the BSP-BJP coalition government.

Two new regional parties were born—Loktantrik Congress Party and Jantantrik Bahujan Samaj Party, which after muscling their way in the coalition governments had ultimately disintegrated and disappeared from UP's political landscape.

The Shiv Sena, though a regional party, had the wherewithal to save the party from a split. After all, they were sitting in power.

Uddhav fought a lonely battle though he was heading a coalition government. He did not alert or activate his seasoned partners, NCP in Mumbai and the Congress in Delhi. A combined and coordinated effort could have made some noise in the right quarters, despite the much-talked about involvement of the powerful BJP leaders in the coup.

People who had seen Shiv Sena's rise recall how Bal Thackeray, after declaring his successor, had made fervent appeals to the party cadres to support his son Uddhav and his grandson Aditya. He had invoked the party's values of faith and loyalty to safeguard Shiv Sena from damage, as his nephew, Raj Thackeray, was gearing up to raise a banner of revolt.

However, Uddhav's emotional pitch to the people not only came late in the day but failed to stir Shiv Sainiks into action. After his resignation on 30 June 2022, he said he is not the one to stick to power and see the blood of Shiv Sainiks spill on the roads of Mumbai.

Subsequently, the matter reached the Election Commission

of India, which also declared Eknath Shinde's faction as the real Shiv Sena and allotted the party's symbol of bow and arrow to him.

The old and original Shiv Sena, founded by Bal Thackeray, not only lost power, but the party title and symbol, too. His supporters shed tears, but it was too late to save the party from its biggest vertical split, as power attracts numbers when loyalty loses its glue.

The Tiger's son had conceded defeat, which many believed was strategic.

Maharashtra had two Shiv Senas, the *asli* and the *naqli*.

Another regional party was born.

The dust had not fully settled when the BJP targeted the NCP, founded by the tallest Maratha leader of the state, Sharad Pawar in 1999, and succeeded in splitting both the party as well as the family.

The one who stabbed Sharad Pawar in the back was his own nephew Ajit Pawar, whom he had groomed along with his daughter Supriya Sule to take the party forward when he wouldn't be around.

Ajit Pawar took away forty-one of the fifty-three party MLAs, who attended the meeting convened by him, while only eleven attended Sharad Pawar's rival meeting.

It is not clear whether Sharad Pawar ever shared or discussed his succession plan with anyone or not. But people in the know of the developments always believed that the senior Pawar was training his nephew Ajit for a state role and daughter Supriya for a national role. But when it came to anointing his successor, he opted for his daughter Supriya Sule and declared her heir apparent in June 2023. She, along with another senior leader Praful Patel, were appointed working presidents.

Ajit Pawar was stunned. He sulked as he felt let down by his uncle for whom he had toiled hard, executing all decisions, taken by the senior Pawar, good, bad or ugly.

Everyone knew about BJP's political ambitions in Maharashtra and about its roaring 'washing machine,' which cleaned defectors of their corrupt deeds and charges. Ajit too was facing corruption cases and was under the scanner of central agencies.

At a BJP booth workers' meeting in Bhopal in the run up to the 2024 General Elections, Prime Minister Narendra Modi had dubbed NCP as 'Naturally Corrupt Party,' involved in corruption worth Rs 70,000 crore. He had also urged BJP workers to uncover more scams and increase NCP's 'scam meter.' Modi had specifically mentioned Ajit Pawar and his involvement in the irrigation scam.

But when Ajit Pawar jumped ship, the BJP rewarded him as well as other defectors from Shiv Sena and NCP with reprieves. *The Indian Express* of 4 April 2023, reported:

> Twenty-three of the twenty-five prominent opposition leaders, facing action from central agencies for alleged corruption, have moved to the BJP and got reprieve too since 2014. They included ten from the Congress, four each from the NCP and the Shiv Sena, three from Trinamool Congress, two from TDP, and one each from Samajwadi Party and YSRCP. Barring the Congress, all are regional parties.

The report further stated:

> The latest set of findings show that a bulk of the Central action was focused on Maharashtra through the political turbulence of 2022 and 2023 in the state. In 2022, the Eknath Shinde faction broke away from the Shiv Sena and formed a new government with the BJP. A year later, the Ajit Pawar faction

broke away from the NCP and joined the ruling NDA coalition. Records show that cases faced by two top leaders of the NCP faction, Ajit Pawar and Praful Patel, were subsequently closed. In all, 12 prominent politicians from Maharashtra are on the list of 25, eleven of whom switched to the BJP in 2022 or later, including four each from NCP, Shiv Sena and Congress.

The NCP had become vulnerable as Ajit Pawar, who handled his uncle's 'political laundry,' was fuming and fretting. Quick to take advantage, the BJP found the ground ripe to implement its mischievous plan.

The BJP wanted support of more lawmakers to numerically strengthen the Shinde government as a case of disqualification of sixteen Shiv Sena MLAs was pending in the Supreme Court.

Political commentators say the BJP also wanted to cover more geographical areas electorally in a state where leaders' influence is often confined to their respective regions, one of which was Western Maharashtra, the NCP stronghold.

They dangled the carrot and Ajit Pawar grabbed it for succour from cases as well as for power.

Consequently, yet another regional party was created in Maharashtra to which the old and the original NCP lost its symbol.

Sharad Pawar remained unmoved even as people kept guessing his next move. Splits and breakups were not new to him as he himself was a pioneer of the same. At one of the workers' meetings, he had recalled the split in his party in 1980.

He had then told the media, 'We had fifty-eight lawmakers and were left with six only. The party rebounded and in the next assembly elections, the strength of our MLAs went to sixty-nine with only four deserters managing to win the elections again.'

Was it a warning to the rebels who broke the party at the

time when he was in his twilight years? Or is there any substance in speculations that he himself sent Ajit Pawar to the BJP camp to save and secure his joint family business?

The fact is, Sharad Pawar lives politics. He knows the state, its politics, and its leaders, like the palm of his hand. People were always in awe of the maverick politician, who could make or mar the future of lawmakers. But he was flexi in politics and had more friends and no foes.

The tallest Maratha leader had done fairly well in the 2019 assembly elections playing on the Maratha pride in the campaign. Maharashtra has about thirty-five per cent Maratha voters, and in stature, Ajit Pawar and Eknath Shinde are pygmies before Sharad Pawar.

But in 2023, he looked frail and was visibly hurt by his nephew's taunt, 'Some, even in their 80s, are not willing to retire. People in Maharashtra retire at the age of 58 in government jobs, most people stop their active professional life at 75 years, but there are a few who while touching 84 are not willing to retire.'

Pawar loyalists did not take Ajit's words kindly, while senior Pawar worked hard, defying age and ailment, to rebuild the party with public support and to 'teach a lesson' to his detractors in the 2024 General elections. Prime Minister Narendra Modi had described him as a wandering soul.

Pawar refused to engage in a war of words. Instead, he focused on winning seats. He had invested his entire life in nursing his constituency and was confident his supporters would not desert him, even if the opponent is all-mighty and had pecuniary powers.

The result of the 2024 General Elections for forty-eight Lok Sabha seats came on expected lines as the public rejected the BJP's formula to win Maharashtra. It could win only nine seats, while Shiv Sena (Shinde) managed seven and NCP (Ajit) only one seat.

On the other hand, Congress won thirteen, Shiv Sena (UBT) nine and NCP (Sharad Pawar) eight seats. One seat went to an Independent.

As against a total of seventeen of BJP led-NDA, the Congress-led INDIA bloc won thirty seats, pouring cold water on BJP's dreams of ruling the state a few months later. Raj Thackeray, whom the BJP befriended before the Lok Sabha polls to confuse Shiv Sainiks, failed to deliver, though he had not only shared the dais with the Prime Minister, but was also showered with much adulation and accolades.

Journalist and author Girish Kuber brilliantly summed up the poll results after the rout of the BJP-led NDA in the 2024 general elections.

> The outcome in Maharashtra underscores three points. One, the BJP's remarkable ability to score self-goals, two, its exceptional ineptitude in understanding Sharad Pawar's skills in bringing all those who matter together for political gains and three, Uddhav Thackeray rising to the challenge and displaying an as-yet-unseen elasticity in political manoeuvrings. (*Indian Express*, 8 June 2024)

BJP's move backfired. but the party leadership did not give up till they won the 2024 Assembly polls a few months later and decimated both Shiv Sena (UT) and NCP (SP) in October 2024.

In a turn of events, Devendra Fadnavis became CM and Shinde his deputy CM. Shinde reluctantly accepted the position after holding the government formation for several days. He continues to sulk and does not share cordial relations with CM Fadnavis. Shinde may soon turn into a small player in times to come. He has already upset the BJP high command

> by his silent drama of protest against his demotion from CM to Deputy CM. Mistrust prevails between them.
>
> NCP leader Ajit Pawar also became deputy CM for the fifth time. 'I want to become chief minister one day and implement my own plans for the state,' Pawar said. (Abhinay Deshpande in *Hindu* on 9 July 2023)

The four regional parties are here to stay for a long time to come—or till the time the BJP sees utility in them. The bi-polar state is packed with parties to manipulate.

***

How regional parties are born

Maharashtra'a latest story answers it lucidly.

In 2010, a Marathi film called *Zenda* (flag) had become a great hit as its storyline had elements from Raj Thackeray's life—from his exit from the Shiv Sena in 2005 to the formation of the Maharashtra Navnirman Sena.

The story revolved around two party workers who decided to part ways, with one going with the leader who formed a new party. The film covered the drama that followed, leaving party workers befuddled and the public betrayed, amid a heavy exchange of allegations and counter allegations.

The film has become a reality today.

If politics is one big theatre, then the city of glitz and glamour has not failed in producing such thrillers, depicting elections with multiple heroes and villains chasing *shakti*, power, leaving the audience more confused than erudite about the 'real and the surreal.'

Ahead of the Assembly elections in November 2024, there was confusion galore in Maharashtra, as established regional parties founded by maverick leaders fell like a pack of cards and leaders switched loyalties for power or protection. People usually have more interest in electing their government in the states than at the Centre, as the saying goes, *Dilli toh door hai*!

The voters were confused, as their loyalties were with the original parties, Shiv Sena (UBT) and NCP (Sharad Pawar), though both had a new symbol and name. The voters were also disgusted as their elected representatives had betrayed and joined another party.

Leaders are not only choosy about their party symbols but possessive too. After all, election symbols are the face of the party. The battle is half lost if the symbols are changed, that too a few months before the General Elections, like in Maharashtra. But Uddhav Thackeray and Sharad Pawar were determined to turn the tables on their detractors.

Social media bailed them out in propagating their symbols ahead of the Lok Sabha elections. The candidates spent more time, money and energy in telling the voters about their symbols than their issues. Shiv Sena (UBT), launched 'Mashal Geet,' a music video popularising the party's new symbol of a Flaming Torch. Similarly, NCP leader Sharad Pawar unveiled the party's new symbol (man-blowing *tutari*) at an event held at Raigad Fort in February 2024. By the time assembly elections were held, many knew about their new symbols.

The results were a shocker. The BJP led Mahayuti, which had suffered losses in the Lok Sabha polls, had a landslide victory four months later. Both Shiv Sena(UT) and NCP(SP) were decimated in November 2024. The Congress leadership described the results as 'unexpected' and a result of 'targeted manipulation.' They also questioned the jump in the voters list since the General Elections.

Regional parties are born out of several premises

First, a public movement like creation of a separate state ends in the formation of a party like in Jharkhand, Uttarakhand and Telangana.

Second, ambitious leaders break parties and head a faction. Like NCP in Maharashtra; Trinamool Congress in West Bengal.

Third, caste loyalties propel leaders to form their separate parties like Rashtriya Janata Dal in Bihar and Samajwadi Party and Bahujan Samaj Party in UP.

Most of them fight succession battles.

Sometimes, I wonder how can an original party be deprived of its identity when the founder president is alive, petitioning to one and all.

How could the Election Commission of India declare the breakaway faction of NCP as real, allowing it to use the party name and symbol of clock, signalling timeout for its founder Sharad Pawar? Could justice be so blind? A better way would have been to freeze the symbol till the dispute was settled.

And if the Election Commission continues to recognise splinter groups as the real ones, then there is no way to check the proliferation of new regional parties. Some say, they blackmail for power and pelf. But then those in power, whether the Congress or the BJP, also bribe them for support on the floor of the house or in elections.

Bringing up a party is like rearing a child, until and unless it has been formed for a limited purpose of contesting an election. Then why should splits be hurriedly recognised, even if the numbers are in their favour!

The power and impact of regional parties has been recognised by researchers from time to time. Milan Vaishnav wrote the following in an article in November 2013.

> The exponential increase in the number of parties contesting elections, particularly over the past two decades, and the shrinking margins of victory in parliamentary elections are direct results of the emergence of new regional power-centres. Their rise has indisputably transformed the very nature of electoral politics in India. For the foreseeable future, it is unimaginable that a single party could form the government in New Delhi—a testament enough to this tectonic shift.

The BJP did change the scenario for a decade by getting a majority in the Indian Parliament in 2014 and 2019. But five years later, it fell short of the majority mark and solicited support of two regional parties—JD(U) and Telugu Desam Party.

Founder-Director of the Centre for Voting Opinion &Trends in Election Research (C-Voter) Yashwant Deshmukh explains their birth and growth.

'The Congress has not polarised all anti-BJP votes. That is why 15-20 per cent bloc of anti-BJP votes goes to the regional parties. Be it anti-Congress or anti-BJP, the regional party's strength is because the Congress is perceived as weak. If Congress starts gaining, it is unlikely it would gain at the expense of the BJP, but would largely gain at the cost of the regional parties. This is why regional parties are never keen to give a scope to the Congress beyond a point to gain traction. They know if Congress gains beyond a point, their vote would shift largely to the grand old party. There would always be a seat sharing issue in an opposition (non-BJP bloc) as the Congress gets aggressive after getting oxygen—ask for more seats, regional parties not keen to leave more seats.'

As Congress and Regional Parties sit on a see-saw, the BJP finds its slogan of Congress *Mukt Bharat* fading behind the glow of satraps in states.

Chapter 2

Regional Parties are Running the Show

28 May 1996: Former Prime Minister Atal Bihari Vajpayee was replying to a debate on the trust vote moved against his thirteen-day-old government in the Lok Sabha.

The astute politician knew his government would collapse as party managers had failed to secure support of other parties in the post-demolition era and his BJP had managed to win just 161 of 543 seats in the Indian Parliament.

The BJP had become a political untouchable after the demolition of the Babri Mosque in Ayodhya on 6 December 1992. No political party was willing to partner with the BJP, even for power when the nation was in the grip of an intense debate on secularism vs. communalism.

Recalling an incident from his exhaustive political diary to reinforce the importance of cordial relations between the ruling and the opposition parties in a parliamentary democracy, Vajpayee in his inimitable style had told the house, 'As an opposition leader, Prime Minister Narasimha Rao had sent me to UN Convention in Geneva to put across India's point of view. Pakistanis were shocked and asked how it was that I was there.'

Vajpayee concluded his speech with, '*Sarkare Aayengi, Jaayengi, Partiyan Banegi, Bigarengi, Magar Yeh Desh Rehna Chaiye.*' ('Governments will come and go, political parties will break and dissolve but the country should survive.')

His advice to both the ruling and the opposition parties went unheeded as the communication lines between them had started breaking down. He lost the confidence motion and became the country's Prime Minister for the shortest duration of thirteen days.

Again in 1999, his thirteen-month-old government lost a no-confidence motion by one vote. The perpetrator behind his fall was a regional party, the All India Anna Dravida Munnetra Kazhagam (AIADMK).

Twenty-seven years later, on 28 May 2023, when the new Parliament building in New Delhi, the seat of democracy, was thrown open to the public amid boycott by twenty of the twenty-five opposition parties in the country, Vajpayee was not alive. His words echoed but there were no takers, both in the treasury and the opposition benches. The political rivals had by then turned enemies.

The opposition group had accused the government of constitutional impropriety, demanding that President Droupadi Murmu should preside over the inaugural ceremony instead of Prime Minister Narendra Modi.

In a joint statement, nineteen opposition parties said, 'The President was not only the Head of the State, but also an integral part of the Parliament as she summons, prorogues and addresses it.... In short, Parliament cannot function without the President. Yet, the Prime Minister has decided to inaugurate the new Parliament building without her. This undignified act insults the high office of the President, and violates the letter and spirit of the Constitution. It undermines the spirit of inclusion which saw the nation celebrate its first woman Adivasi President.'

However, they added that they were open to sinking their differences and marking this occasion.

Did the Prime Minister initiate any dialogue to break the impasse? Perhaps not. The Parliamentary Affairs Minister made frail attempts to placate the opposition. The home minister later addressed a press conference in which he denounced them and their act, saying, 'All parties had been invited for the function but they will act according to their feelings.'

The historic ceremony took place in the absence of an opposition, headed by the grand old Congress party that gave the country its first Prime Minister and also ruled it for several decades. Others were regional parties, some of them from ruling states.

Only five from the opposition camp had attended the special event. The Prime Minister said, 'Some dates become the indelible signature on the face of time. 28 May 2023 is one such day.'

The day also marked the complete breakdown of communication lines between the lawmakers who grace the treasury and the opposition benches in Parliament.

Significantly, on the same day, while addressing the Chief Ministers of the BJP-ruled states, the Prime Minister reminded the people about the formation of the National Democratic Alliance on 15 May 1998 and called for celebrations as it had completed twenty-five years.

The architect and first chairman of NDA was the BJP stalwart and most respected leader Atal Bihari Vajpayee, whose first two governments had lasted 13 days and 13 months due to regional parties asserting themselves in hung houses.

The NDA was formed with a single-point mission to keep the Congress out of power and bring regional parties on board.

Initially, it had about twenty-odd members which went to the polls together in 1999, and managed to form the government, too.

It was a fluid scenario, as the numbers of allies kept changing with the exit and entries of regional parties. Vajpayee fought hard to save his tottering government, using his manoeuvring skills, virtually rope-walking. The government managed to complete its full five years only because of Vajpayee's political sagacity.

Both Atal Bihari Vajpayee and Narendra Modi have been charismatic mass leaders, who grew up in the RSS uniform, but their style of functioning is strikingly different. Vajpayee was famous for his political jocularity as well as courtesies, while Narendra Modi is better seen as officious, who took on his detractors with vengeance. Comparisons between the two were consistently drawn within BJP circles as Modi's authoritarian style of functioning became increasingly evident with time.

Soon, all comparisons between the two leaders stopped for two reasons: the generational gap between the two powerful BJP leaders and Modi's constant deliveries on the political turf since 2014. After the party's repeat performance in the 2019 Lok Sabha elections, Modi became a cult, while Vajpayee had remained a mascot.

The decade of Modi's rule saw the government manipulating or mauling the errant regional parties. The BJP's motto was—lure them or break them.

Five years later, in the 2024 Lok Sabha elections, an overconfident Modi gave an ambitious call for 400-plus seats out of a total of 543 seats in Parliament. Despite a historic third term, he failed in his mission of a brute majority.

Stopping him in the tracks was not the grand old Congress, but the rising regional parties.

Political analyst and Founder Director of C-Voters, Yashwant

Deshmukh had repeatedly reeled out the telling numbers in the 2024 General Elections, highlighting how BJP was in a direct contest with the Congress on barely 200 seats.

On the other hand, it was in straight or one-on-one conflict with regional parties in 243 seats. In the remaining 100 seats, the BJP was not in the fight at all.

In 2024, the BJP clearly faced a stiffer challenge from the regional forces than the Congress it had set out to eliminate from the country's political map.

The results started trickling in on 4 June 2024, crashing the BJP's dreams of a landslide win with 400 seats or more. Instead, Narendra Modi and NDA fell thirty-two seats short of the magical majority figure and needed political crutches to run a third consecutive term.

Amid many smirks, people again invoked Modi's comparison with Vajpayee and his coalition dharma that he had adhered to between 1996 and 2004, while heading multiple coalition governments that lasted from thirteen days to over six years.

The question asked was: Will the electoral setback force Modi to show humility, after enjoying a free run for a full decade? He did head an NDA government but the BJP had a comfortable majority, turning regional players into meek partners.

But now the regional parties were back with a vengeance, with enough room to flex their muscles.

The political crutches came from Andhra Pradesh in south and Bihar in north, but their leaders, Chandrababu Naidu and Nitish Kumar, were infamous for their mercurial and intemperate political temperaments. While the BJP alone had 240 members, Naidu's Telegu Desam Party (TDP) brought support of a miniscule sixteen and Nitish Kumar of Janata Dal (U) gave the support of twelve MPs. But in a numerical game, every vote and seat matters, and who else would know it better than the party, which had once lost power for want of one vote.

Both Naidu and Kumar were CMs of their respective states and had huge hunger for funds—Naidu wanted special funds, while Nitish Kumar was seeking special status for Bihar.

In the annual budget presented by Finance Minister Nirmala Sitharaman on 23 July 2024, both these parties got their pound of flesh in lieu of their support to the Central Government as they were obliged with special packages for the development of their respective states.

In a politically prudent move, Sitharaman, donning an off-white silk saree spruced up with Madhubani art and fish motifs, announced a bonanza for poll bound Bihar in her 2025 annual budget. The BJP high command, eyeing an electoral win in Bihar and Andhra Pradesh, has been desperate to upstage the two regional parties JD(U) and RJD, that has been at the helm of affairs for long. Polls in Andhra Pradesh are still far away.

In addition to TDP and JD(U), the BJP led NDA had thirty-two partners, many of whom have been fellow travellers since the formation of NDA in 1998.

Three new prominent members were the untested ones—Shiv Sena (Eknath Shinde), Nationalist Congress Party (Ajit Pawar) and Rashtriya Lok Dal (Ajit Singh). Had BJP not broken the parties, its dream of a third term would have gone *phut*.

Against this, the Opposition bloc I.N.D.I.A won 234 seats, to which the Congress contributed ninety-nine members. The Independents had won seven and non-affiliated parties nine seats. The rest were grabbed by regional forces.

The NDA had ruled India from 1998 to 2004 and had managed to keep its allies in good humour. The BJP returned to power in 2014 and again in 2019 with a clear majority, but decided to share power with its pre-poll partners.

However, in 2024, it needed support of member-parties of NDA, besides the two political crutches, to stake claim to government formation.

When the time came to form the government, members hard-bargained for berths in the Council of Ministers. As Modi was forced to become more accommodative, allies with even one or two MPs found entry into his 72-member Council of Ministers.

What was marketed exclusively as *Modi Sarkaar* for ten years became an NDA government in its bid to acknowledge the contribution of its allies.

That's the power of regional parties and nothing befits their political dreams more than a coalition arrangement! Their growth stems from the power they wield. After all, power begets power.

Perhaps even a strong Prime Minister like Narendra Modi can feel and fret it most today as he has to balance his every act and action.

The United Progressive Alliance, in its reincarnation as the Indian National Developmental Inclusive Alliance (I.N.D.I.A) had 234 members in the Lok Sabha, the bulk having come from the Congress. The other parties with major share in the Opposition bloc were Samajwadi Party with thirty-seven members, Trinamool Congress with twenty-nine, DMK with twenty-two, Shiv Sena (Uddhav Thackeray) with nine and NCP Sharad Pawar with eight seats.

Another dozen-odd parties had their representation in the Lok Sabha in ones and twos. Of them, Aam Admi Party (AAP) and Jharkhand Mukti Morcha (JMM) had governments in Delhi and Jharkhand respectively. The other notable regional parties were Lalu Prasad Yadav's Rashtriya Janata Dal, National Conference and People's Democratic Party of Jammu and Kashmir.

There are sixteen other MPs who do not owe allegiance to either the NDA or to I.N.D.I.A.

In a nutshell, the strength of the regional parties in a house of 543 is around 200. They also rule fifteen states, including Union Territories, independently or in alliance with one of the national parties. Of the national parties, the Congress rules three states, BJP twelve and CPM and AAP, one state each.

After the formation of the government, Modi lay low for the first two months, while Union Defence Minister Rajnath Singh, who had not only inherited Vajpayee's Lok Sabha constituency of Lucknow, but also his cordial style of functioning, became the arbitrator.

However, soon enough, Modi was back to his original form as he supplanted Lok Sabha losses within five months with spectacular wins in Haryana and Maharashtra state assemblies, eclipsing BJP's losses in Jharkhand as well as in Jammu and Kashmir.

Modi decimated regional parties in Haryana, the Indian National Lok Dal (INLD) and its splinter group, Jannayak Janta Party (JJP), founded by former deputy Prime Minister Devi Lal. They had contested the elections with separate alliance partners, INLD with the Bahujan Samaj Party and JJP with Azad Party.

Arvind Kejriwal's AAP, flying high after winning the neighbouring state of Punjab in 2022, also floundered.

The BJP's win in Maharashtra was critical to their political plans as the state is not only the financial capital of the country, but also home to its ideological parent, the Rashtriya Swayamsevak Sangh (RSS), with its headquarters in Nagpur.

Modi believes in advance planning to win battles, disclosed Andhra Pradesh Chief Minister Chandrababu Naidu, while addressing the *Hindustan Times* summit in Delhi on

16 November 2024. 'He has already planned for 2029 General Elections. That is how he works, like a mission,' Naidu said.

The blueprint for Maharashtra must have, therefore, been readied soon after Shiv Sena leader Uddhav Thackeray parted ways with its oldest ally, the BJP, primarily to occupy the CM's chair as well as to protect its prime position and the Hindutva space in the state from encroachment by the BJP. Thackeray could last on the chair till June 2022.

The BJP's strategy was simple—to weaken them and then break them. This could not have been implemented without meticulous planning, secrecy and smart brinkmanship. After an initial setback in the Lok Sabha polls, the *Mahayuti* (grand alliance) is back in power in Maharashtra.

What next for Uddhav and Sharad Pawar? While struggling to pick up the pieces of their completely mauled parties, they are sending mixed signals. Sharad Pawar spoke kindly about RSS appreciating 'their hard work,' while Uddhav Thackeray called on Chief Minister Fadnavis.

Their moves are canny enough to keep both the deputy chief ministers Eknath Shinde and Ajit Pawar on tenterhooks, as well as to retain their flock together. As of now, their MPs and MLAs are staring at a five-year long hiatus, and in some, may have opened channels with the politically savvy Devendra Fadnavis.

Meanwhile, the Chanakyas in the BJP must be readying the party's plan to augment the BJP numbers and reach the majority mark in Parliament. It's not a tall order and could be executed before the two formidable allies withdrew their support to the government. When and how is everyone's guess!

The Fadnavis government does not need support from any quarter to survive in the State Assembly, but Prime Minister Narendra Modi would prefer to fearlessly run without crutches.

The two regional parties, which the BJP had mercilessly broken and weakened to win Maharashtra, can bring seventeen MPs on board. In addition, there are sixteen MPs—nine from small parties and seven Independents—who are not aligned to NDA or UPA. Some may cross over from the opposition to the treasury benches, perforce or by choice.

But the billion-rupee question? Why would Shiv Sena (UT) and NCP (SP) bail out Modi at the Centre? The only possible reason is Pawar's desire to see his daughter Supriya Sule in power at the Centre. But there is also the view that Pawar will not dump his ideology for power. Moreover, he does not trust the BJP. As of now, it's back to rebuilding the party from scratch.

It may be *Gharwapsi* for the Shiv Sena, but at a price. They may demand Shinde's sacrifice. Once he goes, the party will reunite and the Thackerays will be back as the original Shiv Sena. Some backroom manoeuvrings indeed!

Political observers say the Maharashtra story speaks volumes about the use and abuse of regional parties.

Every state has its own tale of sacrifice and sufferings, but these regional parties are here to stay till the two national major parties, the BJP and the Congress, develop their exclusive pan-India base. As of now, they are the two pivots or pillars for the smaller parties to rally around in a give-and-take relationship.

The regional parties have been dominating the politics of some crucial states for more than a decade, which include Uttar Pradesh, Bihar, Maharashtra, West Bengal, Tamil Nadu, Karnataka, Andhra Pradesh, Odisha and Kerala. Each of these states accounts for twenty to eighty Lok Sabha seats, totalling 313 in a house of 543.

Little wonder then that they are courted in every election by the two mainline parties, irrespective of their hold in any one constituency.

Then there are states where regional parties have not found enough space to develop. These include Gujarat, which has been BJP's bastion for decades, Madhya Pradesh, Rajasthan, Himachal Pradesh and Uttarakhand. The few regional parties, which surfaced and sustained in these states are struggling on the fringes.

***

Why support regional parties?

I read this brilliant quote in the media some years back: 'Regional aspiration is the womb of regional parties.' It has stayed with me as these simple words best elucidate the mushrooming growth of regional parties across India with national parties failing to address the cultural, social and ethnic issues of regions, irrespective of their geographical distance from Delhi.

Then there are also demands for greater autonomy and statehood, especially from backward regions hungry for development.

Here are two examples:

The Uttarakhand Kranti Dal (UKD) fought relentlessly for the creation of a separate hill state since its inception in 1979. By the mid-1980s and the 1990s, it became a public movement as people felt the leaders ruling Uttar Pradesh did not understand the issues that troubled them. As an example, they often quoted the parameters used for the creation of administrative blocks in the hill districts, copied from the pattern used for the plains and ignored the difference that existed in their ecology, climate and terrain of the two.

Interestingly, there were cabinet ministers as well as a Chief Minister in undivided Uttar Pradesh from the four hill districts in the region, but somehow, they too overlooked the requirements of a hilly region, while approving faulty plans. They joined the UKD movement and a separate state became a reality.

Uttarakhand, which for many years was also called Uttaranchal, was created in November 2000. The BJP and the Congress locked horns over its name and capital, more than the development plans and the funding for the new state.

UKD soon became politically irrelevant after it failed to win elections.

Telangana was also carved out of Andhra Pradesh in 2014 after an over-decade long agitation by the Telangana Rashtra Samiti (TRS) founded by Chandra Shekhar Rao in 2001, with a one-point mission to get statehood for Telangana.

People voted TRS to power in the very first election of the new state in 2014. Rao ruled the state for a decade till 2023, after which his aspirations to rule the country or play a significant role in national politics grew. He renamed TRS as Bharat Rashtra Samiti (BRS) in 2022. However, Rao lost the 2023 State Assembly election and failed to win even a single seat in the 2024 Lok Sabha polls. His national dreams had to be shelved.

A considerably weakened BRS sits in the opposition today, while the Congress rules the state and the BJP, after winning eight seats in the 2024 Lok Sabha elections, works steadily to expand its footprint in the state. However, BRS, which is trying to revert to its original name TRS, may be down but not out.

Statehood demands are now emerging from different corners of the country and there are experts who support smaller states for better administration and governance. The long pending demands include creation of Vidarbha in Maharashtra, Saurashtra in Gujarat, Bodoland in Assam, Gorkhaland in North Bengal, besides division of Uttar Pradesh into four states and so on. The agitations go on in UP and Maharashtra.

While regional parties continue public movements to demand statehood, no central government would touch the hot issue with a barge pole. Undoubtedly, the regional parties represent regions, advocate their developmental priorities, linguistic and cultural issues, watch regional imbalances, while they also work as pressure groups, arm twist and sometimes blackmail the government at the Centre.

There is also a give and take as witnessed recently in Maharashtra where the BJP leadership rewarded Ajit Pawar with deputy chief ministership for breaking NCP, founded by his uncle Sharad Pawar, and by simply ignoring the accusations of corruption made against him by none other than Prime Minister Narendra Modi himself.

National parties have failed to develop leadership at the state level as the central leadership has perhaps suffered from insecurities of getting overshadowed or overthrown by them.

The Gandhi family dominates the Congress till date with few popular or powerful leaders left at the state level to galvanise units. As the Gandhi scion appeal is also restricted, unlike their grandmother Indira Gandhi, who was as popular in North as in South, the Congress struggles with their revival plans.

The BJP, which has pursued charges of nepotism against Congress with an undying vengeance, also fell for cult worship after Narendra Modi arrived on the scene and took the country by storm with his addictive cocktail of development and Hindutva.

Initially, the BJP did try to cultivate mass leaders at the state level, especially in the North—Vasundhara Raje Scindia in Rajasthan, Shivraj Singh Chauhan in Madhya Pradesh and Yogi Adityanath in Uttar Pradesh, till they became a threat to the central leadership.

Incidentally, both the BJP and the Congress failed to spread and secure their base in Southern India as they were viewed as Hindi speaking parties. They did not groom local leadership and some who grew popular were shunted out.

The Congress failed to retain its post-Independence hold on these Southern states by losing ground to popular leaders, many of whom came from the glamour industry. Now, we see both the national parties desperately trying to penetrate in the regions by riding piggyback on the regional parties, who protect their fiefdoms fiercely.

Brief history of regional parties

From 1952 to 1967, the Congress had comfortably ruled Independent India as the opposition parties till then were fragmented and feeble. However, its hegemony was first challenged after the death of the country's first Prime Minster Jawaharlal Nehru in 1964.

While the Congress continued to retain power at the Centre by winning 283 seats in the 1967 General Elections, it failed to win majority in seven states. The Opposition formed coalition governments in the states of Uttar Pradesh, Punjab, Haryana, Madhya Pradesh, Bihar, West Bengal, Orissa, Madras and Kerala, proving to be a big turning point in Indian politics. Regional parties not only registered their presence in the battleground, but also became shareholders in some states.

Thereafter, as political turbulence rocked the country and the Congress, regional parties started surfacing across India, some protesting against the control of the party and the government by an autocratic Indira Gandhi. She ruled the country till 1977, when many small parties led by big leaders came together under the banner of the Janata Party and dealt a deafening defeat to the Congress.

It was the start of the coalition era at the Centre, but their very first experiment failed. The government collapsed under the weight of ambitious heavyweights, including several claimants for the post of Prime Minister. These parties had joined hands to oust Indira Gandhi, and once she had been defeated, they strived for power, pulling down each other in the clamour.

The first government of Morarji Desai completed barely 857 days and Charan Singh ruled for 171 days.

The Congress returned to power in 1980, but the regional parties had tasted blood by then. They also started asserting themselves as their share in Parliament and strength in states started growing.

The 1989 story of Janata Dal is known to all and sundry. The government lasted till mid-1991, despite change of leadership. The second attempt of the opposition failed.

In the subsequent general elections, no single party could attain a majority and regional parties had a ball, as they became crucial to the formation of the Central Government. They shared power and dominated the country's politics till 1998.

Eventually, before the 1999 general elections, the BJP, under the leadership of Atal Bihari Vajpayee, formed pre-poll alliances with about two dozen parties from different regions and branded itself as the National Democratic Alliance. Vajpayee won a comfortable majority in 1999 and ruled the country for a full term of five years.

The Congress, with its partners, founded the United Progressive Alliance. Its new version is I.N.D.I.A.

Regional parties were thus accommodated and awarded by both NDA and UPA in their respective governments at the Centre. The BJP-led NDA ruled the country from 1999-2004 and Congress led-UPA from 2004 to 2014.

Before that the regional parties had also given four PMs to the country, Vishwanath Pratap Singh and Chandrashekhar in 1989-90, and HD Deve Gowda and IK Gujral between 1996-98.

The elevation of Janata Dal leader HD Deve Gowda with forty-six MPs to the PM's chair gave rise to Prime Ministerial ambitions of several regional satraps, as they struggled with the formation of the third and the fourth front at the Centre.

However, the coalition governments proved fragile as the country thrice faced general elections between 1996-1999.

Political analyst and psephologist Yashwant Deshmukh, founder director of C-Voters, recalls the three major landmark years in Indian democracy—1967, 1977 and 1989. These were the years when regional parties had become the principal force against the Congress.

Deshmukh remarked: 'Then the prime orientation of these political parties was anti-Congressism. Today this pole has changed and now they are anti-BJPism. Interestingly, the major chunk of parties in the anti-BJP alliance have had an anti-Congress base or have grown from an erstwhile anti-Congress support base.'

This explains the inherent contradictions in the opposition bloc I.N.D.I.A. Its major members like the NCP, TMC are the splinter groups of Congress, while SP, JD(U), DMK, CPI and CPM have largely grown in anti-Congress boots. They hijacked the traditional vote bank of the Congress, whose revival can be detrimental to their health.

However, while facing an aggressive BJP since 2014, these parties are finding ways to stick together despite their inherent contradictions, to provide a viable platform for anti-BJP votes.

The phenomenon of Narendra Modi has bamboozled them as he changes his strategy in every election in every state, enfeebling opponents with splits and empowering supporters with successes. Milan Vaishnav and Jamie Hintson in their 2019 paper summed up the current political scene as:

> The BJP's victory, spearheaded by the party's Prime Ministerial candidate Narendra Modi, ushered in a debate among political scientists and political analysts over whether the country's electoral politics was experiencing a paradigm shift. Indian politics was synonymous with coalition politics between 1989 and 2014, following decades of Congress Party dominance at the national level; but for that quarter century, no single party was strong enough to earn a parliamentary majority on its own, relying instead on dozens of pre- and post- election allies to form a governing coalition. (*The Dawn of India's Fourth Party System*, Milan Vaishnav and Jamie Hintson, Carnegie Endowment For International Peace)

The answer is straight and simple: The paradigm shift has happened as majority rule has replaced coalition governments. Regional parties will be accommodated not as compulsion but goodwill.

In both 2014 and 2019, the BJP had majority on its own and forming an NDA government was a matter of choice, and not compulsion. Modi ruled as he wished, while allies remained mute spectators.

Why? The BJP is eyeing expansion of its popular vote base in virgin regions while the members enjoyed power.

The regional parties are in demand with every political party courting them and voters counting on them for whatever little they bring on the board, but the question remains: what about their health? Most of these parties were born and reborn between 1960 and 1990.

Modi's decision to continue the NDA came as a blessing in 2024 when the government needed support to form the government.

Now, the government is well-ensconced in power, but paradoxically, regional parties stand at a strange crossroad. While many of them are still young, having been born in the 1990s, their leaders are ageing and ailing, triggering succession wars and splits. Their vulnerability is also being exploited by those eyeing their political space. In addition to this, they also face a challenge of protecting their turf as the BJP is moving aggressively to expand its footprint in these areas.

Interestingly, age has now slowed down the political ambitions of regional satraps. HD Deve Gowda, the founder of JD(S) is ninety-one, Sharad Pawar is eighty-four, and Lalu Yadav is seventy-six.

Chapter 3

Succession is a Family Affair

Succession battles in family-controlled regional parties are usually messy as they often divide both the parties as well as the families. Some politicians were wise enough to successfully script their succession plans during their lifetime.

The three astute politicians—Mulayam Singh Yadav, Lalu Prasad Yadav and Sharad Pawar—floated their respective parties in the 1990s; SP in 1992, RJD in 1997 and NCP in 1999.

Both the Yadav chieftains had flirted with several socialist outfits and briefly with the Congress before parting ways. NCP is a breakaway faction of the grand old party. Comfortably ensconced in their home states of Uttar Pradesh, Bihar and Maharashtra, they have dominated the politics of the country.

Move to South, the transition of legacy in DMK was quite smooth as it was written, acted and directed by its President M Karunanidhi in the political theatre of Tamil Nadu. He was called Kalaignar, the artist in recognition of his rich contribution to cinema and literature and he proved his mettle in the political world too.

Before he drew his succession plan, he often used to dismiss questions on the sensitive issue by saying, 'The DMK is not a Sankara Mutt, where the successor is decided by the pontiff (elder in the family) and not by popular vote. DMK is a democratic political party, believing in participatory politics and respected majority opinion.'

Karunanidhi himself had contested an election to become DMK President after the death of its founder CN Annadurai in 1969, with whom he did not have any familial links.

But when it came to him handing over his legacy to his third son MK Stalin, he declared it to the public, unlike Mulayam Singh Yadav of Uttar Pradesh, who had preferred his actions to speak more than his words.

Thus, when Karunanidhi declared his son as his heir apparent, sometime in 2016, it did not come as a shock or surprise and he explained why he had chosen his younger son over the elder one. This is what he had said, according to a newspaper report:

> It is not a sudden development, suggesting that as in big corporations, such plans in political parties are most successful only if introduced incrementally, preparing workers for the changes—but, once announced, need to be followed through ruthlessly.
>
> ...'When Stalin was very young, he formed the youth wing and worked tirelessly. Then, from the time of MISA (the then draconian preventive detention law) for protesting against the Emergency in 1976 when he went to prison, he has undergone torture, worked by himself and attained the position of the DMK's future leader, step by step. Given this, he is today my political successor. (TE Narasimhan, *Buisness Standard*, 7 November 2016)

Stalin climbed the ladder step by step since becoming the party's general council member in 1973. He was elected mayor of Chennai in 1996 and has contested multiple assembly elections since 1984. He was inducted into the cabinet in his fourth term, appointed deputy CM in 2009, soon after the Lok Sabha elections, and party's working president in 2017. Karunanidhi was ailing by this time and breathed his last in August 2018. Almost naturally, Stalin established himself as an undisputed leader by winning the 2021 assembly elections, the first after his father's death.

Karunanidhi's elder son Alagiri and his supporters were dismissed after violent skirmishes with Stalin's workers. Even before the struggle for accession and Stalin's crowning, Alagiri had shifted his base to Madurai. Alagiri could hardly protest as he lacked Stalin's experience.

Now, the 1953-born Stalin has rolled out his succession plan and as a first step, appointed his actor-politician son Udhayanidhi Stalin as his deputy Chief Minister, soon after the 2024 Lok Sabha elections. He would now groom him for the 2026 Assembly elections in the state. There were some murmurs, but no open dissent followed this announcement. People, in general, have no qualms in accepting a dynast as long as their elected leader delivers.

Most of these regional satraps have big political families with a majority of the members harbouring huge political aspirations. Often, their businesses are also linked with their politics.

As many of these parties were born in the 1990s, their leaders are now ageing or ailing as many of them had floated their independent parties after spending years travelling and testing their fate in other outfits. They soon realised the urgent need to decide their political heir while they were around. Obsessively, their prime concern was the longevity of the precious parties they raised against all odds, and the transfer of their legacy in the hands of their children, who embraced politics as their profession.

None of the four leaders had inherited politics or political parties. They were first-generation politicians but could not resist the temptation of promoting their kith and kin while drawing their succession plans. Clearly, trust has been a major factor which works in favour of the dynasts.

The two satraps from Northern India, Mulayam and Lalu, products of the Mandal movement, belonged to the backward caste and had challenged Brahmin hegemony in their respective regions. Sharad Pawar, a Maratha, the dominant caste in Maharashtra, came from a middle-class agricultural family from Baramati in Pune. Karunanidhi from the South was an intellectual superstar, who defeated his worthy rival to become party president after the death of the party's founder.

Ironically, while neither of them inherited their legacies, they chose to hand over theirs to their families.

Even as Karunanidhi was the most successful of them, his son MK Stalin was also forced to go through the grind. People recall how his father had helped Stalin build his image, independent of his father. He never said, 'I will consult my father,' as and when ticklish issues came up in his work. His father had given him brilliant advisers to help him take wise decisions.

Sharad Pawar was eighty-two years old and Lalu Yadav was seventy-five when they started the succession process in their respective parties. It is an open secret that Supriya Sule and Tejashwi Yadav are their respective political heirs, but their formal coronation is pending. Mulayam, who is elder to them, proved to be the niftiest of all as without splitting his much-treasured party, he handed over his legacy to his son Akhilesh Yadav.

The battle for control of the Samajwadi Party briefly turned ugly, threatening to tear the party apart. However, Mulayam with his Machiavellian skills saved it from a formal split. Tragically, it was his death on 10 October 2022, which reunited the huge family, sealing the narrow divisions and differences that the process caused.

Like Karunanidhi, Mulayam knew his son Akhilesh Yadav was the future of the party, but unlike the southern leader, he could not publicly declare it as he was actually fond of his younger brother Shivpal Singh Yadav, and perhaps feared a split in his party more than the family. The BJP often derides Akhilesh Yadav for having usurped the throne and thrown out his father and uncle from the party they had founded, but SP followers know who was actually behind the succession saga. Mulayam had his own way of pushing his will and wish on others.

The family fought the 2024 Lok Sabha elections together, but also displayed an unusual bonhomie with the message that nothing was more valued than the *Parivar*. Despite all this bonhomie, some lingering doubts about mistrust between the family members may, however, continue to persist.

'Netaji,' as Mulayam was reverentially addressed, orchestrated every move according to his own script with minimum deviations, as a majority of the players were the director's actors. His flip flops often confused the public, partymen and family alike, but he was on an undeclared mission. His political heir needed his blessings for acceptance by the rank and file of the SP, as only Mulayam's writ used to run in the family and the party as long as he lived. It was near impossible for his son Akhilesh Yadav to win the succession battle without his will and support.

How it all started

The Samajwadi Party won its first clear majority in the 2012 UP State Assembly polls, two decades after the party's inception in 1992. Earlier, its founder president Mulayam Singh Yadav had headed a *jugaad* government in 1989, an SP-BSP coalition government in 1993, and again a 'jumbo government of ninety ministers' in 2003.

Mulayam harboured two dreams: first that his party should win a clear majority in the 2012 Assembly polls, and second, that it should get national party status.

The campaign for the 2012 Assembly polls was planned by Mulayam and meticulously executed by his son Akhilesh, who cycled across the length and breadth of the state to bring the party to power. SP won 224 of the 403 seats. Mulayam was thrilled.

The obvious choice for the CM's post was Mulayam, but he had some other plans about which he discreetly deliberated with his trusted friends and family members, academicians and party leaders in Lucknow, Saifai and Delhi.

Mulayam was then seventy-three years old and his concern, if any, was the longevity of the party. He knew there would be opposition to his plan, both from within the family as well as the party, especially from the old guards.

A senior party leader confided, 'Netaji wanted to ensure there was no opposition from Saifai, his home village. Though the villagers believed the son had a rightful claim on his father's legacy, they had a soft corner for his brother Shivpal Singh Yadav as his contribution to the party was immense.'

Mulayam kept his plan close to his chest, but often tested the waters by throwing the issue in the open. He soon realised that there would be no opposition from Saifai to his plan of installing Akhilesh as CM, as he had toiled hard for the party's win in 2012.

He then implemented his gameplan in Lucknow, prompting young and old alike to demand that Akhilesh be the next CM of UP. He knew that no one would dare suggest Akhilesh's name till he prompted them. As the whispers grew louder, Mulayam himself became a dissenting voice.

Often leaders quell the opposition by opposing moves that are initiated at their behest. Mulayam even went on a token hunger fast at home telling one and all, 'The young are in a hurry to take over power,' while he quietly checked with his trusted lieutenants if Tipu (as Akhilesh is addressed at home) would be able to run the government. Mulayam not only told party functionaries, but even his friends to demand that Akhilesh be made CM.

Once they got a whiff of what was going on in his mind, well-wishers including professionals started publicly proposing to him the need for a generational shift in the party. Mulayam's cousin Prof Ram Gopal Yadav was leading the group which supported the move to instal Akhilesh as CM.

On the other hand, Mulayam's younger brother Shivpal, who was also a claimant for the position if his brother was not in the race suggested that Netaji become CM and Akhilesh his deputy, somewhat on the lines of the arrangement in Punjab where the then Shiromani Akali Dal government was headed by Prakash Singh Badal as CM and his son Sukhbir Singh Badal was deputy CM.

In between consultations, Mulayam drove down to Raj Bhavan with his son Akhilesh to stake claim to form the government, but told the governor he would inform the name of the CM later, signalling that he was either still indecisive on the issue or was still ironing out ruffled feathers

However, this trip to Raj Bhavan with Akhilesh was interpreted in several ways. The final result was out on 6 March and Akhilesh was sworn in on 15 March 2012.

This was the first step of Mulayam's succession plan.

Mulayam heaved a sigh of relief. On the eve of the swearing-in ceremony, Mulayam had told me in an interview: 'I am a proud father of a Chief Minister. I am happy, relaxed and confident that Tipu will do a fine job. I have told him that his performance should be matchless in the country.'

Shivpal became cabinet minister with important portfolios. He also continued as the state president of the party.

However, not all was well during the SP's five years in power as, in addition to Akhilesh, the government was run by multiple de-facto CMs—his father Mulayam, two uncles, Shivpal and Ram Gopal, and a senior minister, Mohd Azam Khan.

Tension aggravated a few months ahead of the 2017 State Assembly Elections. This time, it was over the control of the SP.

A close scrutiny of Mulayam's back and forth actions, which many described as his ambivalence, reveal a clear-cut design. Emotionally, he was torn between his brother and son, but politically, he knew a generational shift would take the party forward. He stood with his rebel brother, while handing over the party to his son, who was, however, accused of grabbing it.

As elections were drawing closer, the family feud intensified. While Mulayam continued to play peacemaker, Shivpal and Akhilesh remained in striking mode, removing each other's trusted leaders/ministers from the party and the government. Blaming extraneous influences on family and friends, both Mulayam and Akhilesh kept saying that nobody could break the father-son relationship.

On 15 September 2016, Shivpal resigned from both the posts of state president and cabinet minister. The immediate flashpoint was the sacking/removal of ministers and the chief secretary considered close to Shivpal by CM Akhilesh Yadav. The very next day, on 16 September 2016, Mulayam intervened, reinstated the ministers, and rejected Shivpal's resignation, while warning his son about the possible split in the party, which his uncle's exit could cause.

Mulayam also refrained from declaring Akhilesh as the CM face of the party for the impending 2017 Assembly polls to keep Shivpal in good humour and restrain him from taking any step which could damage the party.

This was done even though Shivpal had, in a public statement, agreed to support Akhilesh's candidature for the CM's post if the party returned to power in 2017.

However, there was no truce in sight as the bone of contention was not the CM's post, but the control of the party and funds.

On 23 October 2016, Mulayam expelled his cousin Ram Gopal Yadav from the party for six years, but reinstated him on 17 November 2016. Angry over ticket distribution, he also expelled Akhilesh for six years on 30 December 2016, evoking public comments like, '*Netaji Kya Kar Rahe hai* (What is Netaji up to), his memory is failing him.'

He reinstated Akhilesh the next day, even though a defiant Akhilesh had earlier in the day held a meeting of the SP legislators, in which 200 of the 229 members had pledged their loyalty to him. This overwhelming support to Tipu, party insiders claim, was possible only because of Netaji's blessings.

At a national convention of the party on 1 January 2017, convened by Ram Gopal Yadav, the party's national executive elected Akhilesh as their new national president, leaving no doubts about Mulayam's tacit support to the developments. Netaji himself was conspicuously absent from the convention.

Coincidentally, Kiranmoy Nanda, SP leader in West Bengal, who moved the resolution to elect Akhilesh as the national president of the party, had moved a similar resolution twenty-five years back proposing Mulayam Singh's name for the same position at the time of the party's formation in 1992.The name was seconded by Kapildeo Singh of Bihar.

When I had asked the party's senior leader Rewati Raman Singh about his presence at the convention that elected Akhilesh, he had told me, 'I called Mulayam in the morning to know if he was going to the convention. He told me to go there as he was getting delayed. But he never came. The resolution was passed peacefully as Shivpal also stayed home with Mulayam.'

Later, when the game was over, Mulayam described the rejig in the party illegal. He claimed he was the national president, Akhilesh the CM and Shivpal the state president.

Apparently, either Shivpal failed to understand his brother's uncanny moves or he lacked the voice to question them.

Some leaders close to Mulayam said that initially he wanted to keep the position of the national president for some time more, but he also knew his succession plan would remain incomplete till Akhilesh took full control of the party. His health was deteriorating and he wanted to complete the process in his lifetime.

Ask anyone in the party today, and they will say Akhilesh was elected national president in 2017 according to Mulayam's plan. They also say that a sulking or gullible Shivpal, Ram Gopal and others acted according to his script.

Mulayam won the first two rounds, but the battle was far from over.

It was now the fight for the party symbol and title as he still feared a split in the party if he let loose his estranged brother.

Mulayam approached the Election Commission on 2 January 2017, a day after Akhilesh was appointed national president in Lucknow, to stake claim on the symbol, but kept talking about unity in the party. He was accompanied by Shivpal, a claimant for his legacy, his friend Amar Singh and others.

While arguing the case, their lawyer referred to the National Convention held in Lucknow in which Mulayam was elevated to the status of a mentor, but without passing any resolution for his removal from the party or party post. Mulayam himself insisted the convention was unconstitutional and as he was the president of the party, the symbol—Cycle—belonged to him.

Their lawyer also challenged the legality of the National Convention called by Prof Ram Gopal Yadav, who had been expelled from the party, but he was quick to dispute the claim, providing the printout of the official Twitter handle of then SP state president, Shivpal announcing the withdrawal of the expulsion letter the next day.

> Ram Gopal Yadav, Akhilesh's lawyer Kapil Sibal along with over two dozen senior MLAs and MPs met the Election Commissioners the next day with six boxes of evidence in support of their claim. It had affidavits of thirty-one members of the national executive, 5,242 party delegates who attended the convention in which Akhilesh was elected National President of the party on 1 January 2017, 195 MLAs, forty-eight MLC's, four MPs and eleven members of the Rajya Sabha, as reported by the media then. Kapil Sibal made it a case of a split, of which the Election Commission had also taken cognizance by asking both the groups to furnish their responses. (Rajeev Kumar in his write up on *LinkedIn*, dated 16 January 2017)

Garnering such a massive support would not have been possible for both Ram Gopal and Akhilesh without Mulayam's push.

There were arguments and counter arguments. Instead of submitting proofs in support of his claim, Mulayam on 9 January 2017 and again on 11 January 2017, appealed for unity in the party. 'There should be no division. Party should remain united,' he reminded everybody.

On 17 January, the ECI granted the 'Cycle' symbol to Akhilesh after applying the 'test of majority,' which is also approved by the Supreme Court. After winning the symbol, Akhilesh walked over to his father's house next door and the photograph of the two together signalled, 'All is well.'

I recently asked Shivpal what transpired in the Election Commission, but he dismissed the question with, 'bygones are bygones, we are a *Parivar*.' After much insistence, he said 'we did not submit an affidavit with evidence of our faction's strength.'

After bagging the Cycle symbol, Akhilesh twice met his father at the latter's residence, who by that time, had come out openly in support of his son. However, treading with caution, the Akhilesh camp had also filed a caveat in the Supreme Court in case the Election Commission's decision was challenged.

During the father-son meeting, Mulayam told Akhilesh to retain about forty candidates selected by his camp.

'Over 90 per cent candidates in both the lists are common. We will finalise the list of candidates soon,' Akhilesh had told reporters during an informal chat at his Kalidas Marg residence in Lucknow the same day.

His priority, he said, was to form the Samajwadi Party government again and he promised to take everyone along with him.

'I will take Netaji along...my relations with him are unbreakable,' he said.

'I was confident that I will get the symbol, Cycle. Little time is left now for the elections. It's a big responsibility,' he added.

Along with the symbol, Akhilesh became the undisputed leader of the Samajwadi Party, and quietly started making changes in the party infrastructure.

Hoardings with pictures of Mulayam-Akhilesh surfaced all over Lucknow the day after the Election Commission's verdict with a cryptic message, '*Loha Tap, Kundan Bhaya* (You have to burn to become precious).'

The SP, under the leadership of Akhilesh, who was educated in Environment Science from a University in Sydney, Australia, entered the electoral arena with a progressive face; someone who loved listening to music and playing sports, but had the full support of his rustic but highly qualified father as well as the organisation.

Interestingly, the SP patriarch smiled even after losing the symbol battle to his son, Akhilesh.

The 2017 elections were fought together, but the game was lost to the BJP. The family tussle had taken a toll.

However, when knives were out against Akhilesh, Mulayam strongly defended him saying no one person could be held responsible for the party's defeat at the hustings. But few days later, he publicly humiliated his son for insulting him and thus losing elections.

Shivpal found the time ripe to ask Akhilesh to hand over the reins of the party back to his father.

In May 2017, a frustrated Shivpal started discussing his plans to float a *morcha* (front). Mulayam countered it saying, 'Nobody in the family wanted the party to split; what will be their gains if the party gets divided? Some elements, both inside and outside the party, were conspiring to break the SP, as it alone can defeat the BJP.'

He demanded to know, 'Which party doesn't face ups and downs, which family doesn't have differences. But I am hurt as I independently raised the party, formed the government within eleven months of its inception. I am sure SP and Yadav family will remain united.'

His most interesting comment was, 'Shivpal will only do what I want him to do and I will always keep him with me.'

The director's voice

On 3 October 2017, a frustrated Shivpal convened a press conference to announce the formation of a secular front in Mulayam's presence. Two days later, the national convention of the party was meeting in Agra.

Mulayam restrained Shivpal from launching a secular front and while addressing the press conference, he instead reprimanded Akhilesh for wrong political decisions. However, after Akhilesh's re-election as national president two days later at the Agra convention, Mulayam-Shivpal, who had once again skipped the crucial party meet, congratulated him on his accomplishment.

Finally, in June 2018, Shivpal's supporters announced formation of a Secular Front, which Shivpal said was not a political outfit.

In August 2018, Shivpal finally managed to form Samajwadi Secular Morcha, later rechristened as Pragatisheel Samajwadi Party. Mulayam feigned ignorance, but decided to talk to Shivpal, while Akhilesh said the rebels were free to go wherever they felt comfortable.

Another regional party with a limited purpose was launched.

The Yogi Adityanath government, which had succeeded the SP government after the 2017 assembly elections, promptly allotted an impressive building to house the office of the Pragatisheel Samajwadi Party (Lohia) (PSP-L) on 29 August 2018, the day the party was formed.

Shivpal's new party contested the 2019 Lok Sabha elections

and lost deposits on fifty-five out of fifty-six seats it had contested. UP has eighty Lok Sabha seats.

The family drama had turned murkier when Shivpal contested against his cousin Prof Ram Gopal Yadav's son Akshay Yadav. Both lost the seat to the BJP as Shivpal took away 90,000 votes, while the victory margin was barely 29,000 votes.

The PSP-L leaders had later claimed that the SP had lost the prestigious Kannauj seat, from where Akhilesh's wife Dimple Yadav had contested, primarily because of PSP-L eating into their votes.

Shivpal was a good catch for the BJP, which started smelling blood in the Yadav family split. They wanted PSP-L to independently fight elections and damage their main opponent, the Samajwadi Party.

Mulayam had once told the workers, 'When everybody thought the Samajwadi movement was over, I founded the Samajwadi Party in 1991. When some of my critics described me as a leader of one or two districts, we formed the government four times and remained in power at the Centre twice. Now, when some leaders have tried to divide the party, they will end in isolation.'

But he continued making efforts to reunite the family and the party.

Thus, while the BJP believed the split in the party was final, diminutive yet doughty Mulayam, despite bouts of ill health at the age of eighty-two, was working out a rapprochement between his 'stubborn' son (as he described Akhilesh once in an interview to *Hindustan Times*) and his brother (who grew up playing politics with him). The conciliatory talks were on for some time with both Akhilesh and Shivpal signalling an alliance between the two parties, if not a merger.

It could well be a coincidence that on 16 December 2021,

when CM Yogi Adityanath was taking a dig at the Yadav scion Akhilesh Yadav in the UP Legislative Assembly, saying, 'We respect our elders and do not throw out our father and uncle from the party,' Mulayam Singh Yadav, the founder president of the Samajwadi Party, was engaged in implementing the final shot of his script that had started with his decision to handover his legacy to his son, perhaps before the 2012 assembly elections.

Insiders indicated that even the SP patriarch had preferred an SP-PSP-L alliance and not a merger as he did not want to unsettle his son, who by then was an established Opposition leader and the main challenger to the ruling BJP for the upcoming elections in 2022. The re-entry of Shivpal could have created blocs and groups within the party that was standing solidly behind Akhilesh.

The three Yadavs have their independent bungalows within a radius of a kilometre in the state capital. Mulayam drove down to his brother's place where Akhilesh too was called for an amicable settlement ahead of the 2022 Assembly polls. Mulayam knew Shivpal could be the spoilsport, which BJP would love to exploit in a keenly contested election. Shivpal was trained by Mulayam in poll management and manipulations and an SP-PSP-L togetherness would solidify the Yadav votes.

Significantly, though the party suffered a split, the over 100-member Yadav family had by and large remained united, displaying bonhomie at family functions. The politicians among them stayed in the SP.

SP lost the 2022 Assembly elections and their patriarch Mulayam on 10 October 2022. A shocked family reunited and when the time came to decide who would inherit Mulayam's Mainpuri Lok Sabha constituency, the family unanimously decided on his favourite *bahu* Dimple Yadav's name.

Shivpal said, 'After Netaji's demise, the family had to ensure the victory of their daughter-in-law as the prestige of both the family and the *samaj* was at stake as Netaji was not around.'

Dimple, who is seen as a unifying force in the huge Yadav family, went to Shivpal's house for his blessings. He blessed her with a comfortable win in Mainpuri.

The Pragatisheel Party was soon wound up and Shivpal became a patriarch who guided Akhilesh in several matters. He launched his son Aditya, who became MP from Budaun in the 2024 Lok Sabha polls in which SP emerged as the third largest party in the country.

In 2023, the entire Yadav family assembled in Saifai for Holi, a tradition started by Mulayam Singh Yadav after winning his first MLA election in 1967. This was the first full reunion of the huge Yadav family after seven years of intense infighting in the family.

Some long-time close associates of Mulayam said he wanted his son to go through the drill since he always believed in the dictum: '*Bina kasht ke adhikar nahin milta. Hamari ladai lambi hai. Isme kasht hai, yatnayen hai kintu safalta avashya hai.* (One doesn't get power without pain. Ours is a long battle full of thorns and sufferings, but our victory is for sure).'

It's ironical that generally the rank and file of parties as well as the public prefer sons and daughters of leaders over others at the time of succession. 'Why do you expect it to be different in politics when in all professions like medical, education and even Bollywood, the legacy is transferred to your blood,' is the common refrain.

Unfortunately, if they have to choose between sons and daughters, their first preference would be the son.

Mulayam knew the generational shift in the party was needed and thus the seniors, many of them, his compatriots, would have to step aside to make room for the new blood. He knew the party would have to transform itself to address the issues of modern India, while keeping its ideological base, intact.

He had once told me, 'I told Shivpal, let's take a backseat now and watch Tipu run the show.'

Mulayam often publicly reprimanded Akhilesh for his actions and decisions. His favourite dialogue was, *'Kya tum aise Sarkar/ party chalaoge'* (Is this how you would run the government), but by the time his end came, he had developed confidence in his son, Tipu. He knew the party would be safe in his hands as Akhilesh may make experimental mistakes like he did during his over five-decade long political journey, he may lose elections, but the party would not wither away or be sold; its interests would not be compromised.

The Yadav family feud turned into the most popular political soap opera that the public loved watching and discussing. The BJP leadership, from Prime Minister Narendra Modi to Chief Minister Yogi Adityanath continue to raise it regularly at every forum—election meetings as well as Vidhan Sabha—to embarrass the family.

Mulayam ensured a happy ending, but it really needed some special skills to save the party from a split in a scenario in which parties are falling like a pack of cards.

Mulayam was not born in a political family, but Choudhury Charan Singh had declared him his political heir, saying politicians should take inspiration from Mulayam's life of *sangharsh* and *sangathan* (struggle and organisational skills). Still, he could not inherit the Lok Dal, a regional party founded by the tallest Jat leader Charan Singh.

Circa 1984: Choudhary Ajit Singh returned to India without any political ambitions. His father and founder president of Bhartiya Lok Dal Charan Singh had already declared Mulayam

Singh Yadav as his political heir.

According to KC Rana's book on Charan Singh, several politicians strongly lobbied against Mulayam Singh and propped up a politically naïve Ajit Singh to take over his father's legacy.

Some well-wishers of the party, however, organised a meeting between Ajit Singh and Mulayam Singh in which it was decided that while Ajit would take up the national position, Mulayam would continue to lead UP. Some were still hell-bent on stonewalling any rapprochement between the two leaders and did not allow even this formula to fructify. In the process, Lok Dal, which was emerging as a national party with wings in several states, split and scattered.

The Lok Dal split into two parts—Lok Dal (A) and Lok Dal (B)—which was headed by Mulayam in UP. He later formed a five-party Revolutionary Front and scripted a chapter in the opposition's unity.

Mulayam had to fight a more violent battle with Ajit Singh, this time to become CM. On 3 December 1989, the MLAs cast their votes amid tension. The numbers went in favour of Mulayam.

The Chanakya must be a contented man in his grave now. Uncle Shivpal is back and talks only about *parivar* and not power. The generational shift is complete as the young Yadavs take charge of politics.

Together, they made headlines in the 2024 Lok Sabha elections winning thirty-seven of the eighty Lok Sabha seats, including the prestigious Ayodhya seat.

When scripts fail

The NCP founder president Sharad Pawar had planned to complete the succession process while he was around.

On 2 May 2023, Sharad Pawar threw a bombshell at

the launch of his autobiography at the YB Chavan Centre in Mumbai's Nariman Point by suddenly announcing his decision to quit from the party's chief post in presence of his wife Pratibha Pawar, daughter Supriya Sule and nephew Ajit Pawar.

The crowds were stunned while the cadres went berserk. They had immediately launched hysterical protests, compelling Senior Pawar to withdraw his decision three days later, while emphasising on the need for a succession plan and new leadership.

Later, on 19 June 2023, when the NCP was celebrating its 25th Founders Day in Delhi, Sharad Pawar announced two working presidents with clearly demarcated areas of operation—Praful Patel and Supriya Sule.

Since then, Praful Patel has joined the other faction of the NCP, leaving Surpriya Sule as its sole working president.

Pawar's nephew retaliated and divided the NCP, and on 2 July 2023 had even joined the Shinde government as deputy CM.

Professor Neeraj Hatekar, an academician based out of Mumbai, while dubbing the resignation drama as scripted, said the senior Pawar perhaps wanted to morally re-establish himself in the party, over and above his nephew Ajit Pawar and senior leader Praful Patel. He had sensed the hidden activities in Ajit's camp. He also knew that the BJP was rattled by the formation of the Maha Vikas Aghadi and feared similar coalitions in other parts of the country ahead of the 2024 Lok Sabha polls.

However, Professor Hatekar disagreed that all this was done to clear the path for Supriya Sule.

'Pawar knows that his daughter is more interested in central politics and in policy-making instead of sitting in Maharashtra and doing 'all the dirty jobs'. Running a party organisation is not easy. Realistically, it may not even work—you cannot run Maharashtra from Delhi. Sharad Pawar may have already started grooming someone from the family's third generation for the party post in Maharashtra,' he added.

There are many others who had visualised Supriya as the party's National President and a senior leader like Jayant Patil as State head.

However, the unsavoury developments in the party may have delayed the coronation of the successor. The division in the party had also truncated the legacy.

Senior journalist Vivek Deshpande was of a clear view that as Supriya Sule was inheriting the party, Ajit Pawar decided to move out as he did not want to play second fiddle to his cousin sister and accept any role assigned to him.

Surendra Jondhale, Professor of Political Science, opined that after the decimation of the NCP in the 2024 Assembly polls, the senior Pawar was now left with two options: First, to wait and watch the behaviour of three allies in the ruling alliance; second could be merger of NCP in its parent party, the Congress, which also lacks a pan Maharashtra leader.

Next to Sharad Pawar, Supriya Sule is the undisputed leader of NCP. She is working President now and will be President after her father is not around.

Supriya and her father are not in a hurry to hold a coronation ceremony as they would not want to antagonise senior leaders, who have been with the NCP since its formation.

Pawar was born in a non-political family and had ten siblings. His father Govindrao Pawar was a middle-class agriculturist, while his mother Shardabai was associated with the Peasants and Workers Party. His siblings had gone into different professions. Sharad Pawar entered politics.

Four members of the Pawar family are in politics—Supriya Sule (daughter) is an MP, Ajit Pawar (nephew) is an MLA and deputy CM in the Fadnavis government, Rohit Rajendra Pawar (nephew's son) ia also an MLA and Sunetra (Ajit's wife), is a Rajya Sabha MP. The third generation scion of the Pawar family, Yugendra Pawar, son of Ajit Pawar's brother Srinivas, had lost the Baramati Assembly constituency to his deputy CM uncle.

Pawar had written in his autobiography, *On My Terms: From the Grassroots to the Corridors of Power*, 'He or she will emerge with time.'

The guessing game is on! The immediate challenge is to reestablish or may be, reunite NCP.

Alas, somewhere his script went wrong. Supriya Sule may lead the NCP, but a truncated faction of it.

Open secret

Lalu Prasad Yadav, a father of nine children—two sons and seven daughters—is absolutely clear and candid about his preference for his sons over his daughters when it comes to handing over his political legacy. And between his two sons, his choice has always been Tejashwi Yadav, who played cricket before playing politics.

Lalu had announced his decision at the National Executive meeting of RJD in 2015 when he had said, 'Let there be no doubt in anybody's mind about a successor in the party; only my son would succeed me. Can you claim ownership of somebody's else's land?'

Some leaders believe the regional parties are their personal property—a company, on which only their children have a claim.

Rajesh Ranjan alias Pappu Yadav, then an RJD MP, had questioned Lalu for his remarks that only his son would be his natural successor.

Lalu had then not named his son but sent a message to his two daughters in politics. Ambitious Misa Bharti, one of the daughters, reacted to Lalu's statement '*Khandan ki virasat bete ko jaati hai*'— 'Sons get the mantle, that's the tradition here.'

A step towards his coronation was taken when the RJD Legislature Party, at its meeting on 1 June 2022, passed a resolution authorising Tejashwi Yadav to take all policy decisions in the future. Both the silent contenders—Tej Pratap Yadav and Misa Bharti—were present at the meeting along with Lalu and his wife Rabri Devi.

It is an open secret that two of Tejashwi's siblings—Tej Pratap Yadav and Misa Bharti—even after his anointment as Lalu's heir apparent—harbour a desire to become their father's political heirs. Interestingly, no one in the party as well as family consider them serious contenders or challengers to Tejashwi.

Almost a decade later, in January 2025, Lalu took another step closer to the coronation of Tejashwi when at the party's national executive meet, he elevated his son's status, bringing him at par with himself, but without the post of party national president.

A resolution was passed authorising Tejashwi to take all decisions related to the party, its symbol, title and ticket distribution. In what would be seen as a major step in transition of power in RJD, the party constitution was amended, enabling Tejashwi to share equal decision-making authority with Lalu Yadav.

Quoting health reasons, Lalu had elevated Tejashwi's position saying that he would take on a greater leadership role and solicited everyone's support.

Shivanand Tiwari, RJD national vice president welcomed the decision as he and many others had been suggesting an ailing Lalu to give all decision-making powers to his son, as the party, people and cadre had accepted Tejashwi as Lalu's successor. There is no confusion whatsoever on that count.

Lalu, struggling with the growing political ambitions of his children, had been waiting for an opportune moment to take the final shot as he was testing the waters at home, trying to diffuse tension that his succession plan may have triggered.

Four of Lalu's nine children are in politics—two sons, Tejashwi and Tej Pratap, and two daughters, Rohini and Misa.

Misa, who won the Lok Sabha election from Patliputra after two successive defeats in 2014 and 2019, is stated to be more ambitious and could secure support of her other siblings, especially Tej Pratap Yadav.

Tej Pratap is mercurial and has been making more news for his eccentricities than his political acumen. He had accepted a cabinet minister's post in the first RJD-JD(U) government led by Nitish Kumar in which his brother Tejashwi was deputy CM. Both were elected to the Vidhan Sabha for the first time in 2015.

> This was not a decision he accepted with grace for the state rumour mill is abuzz with stories as to how he locked up his father in the bathroom when he heard that he was being bypassed as the deputy CM. The health ministry was a consolation prize, and one that was given at the behest of his mother Rabri Devi who is clearly his chief supporter. (Priya Segal, 31 October 2018, in *Scroll*)

She wrote, 'Signs of sibling rivalry came to the fore as soon as the limelight shifted to Tejashwi with Tej Pratap commenting wryly that he had no issues if his younger brother got married first since he was more popular with the girls, being deputy CM.'

Insiders strongly feel Lalu should appoint Tejashwi as national president during his lifetime or else he would leave enough room for the succession battle to turn urgly, if not violent.

RJD, national vice president, Shivanand Tiwari remarks,

'Tejashwi must work hard to bring the party to power in 2025. RJD lost 2024 Lok Sabha polls but much of the blame went to Lalu who had taken major decisions. As such, what is Lalu doing himself? The party could win only four Lok Sabha seats despite Tejashwi's electrifying campaign. His leadership is also established, but Lalu must ensure the party survives.'

Lalu wants to see Tejashwi as CM in 2025. But how? 'RJD will have to implement the UP formula, in both letter and spirit to win support of other castes besides M-Y (Muslim-Yadav),' is the common view. In the State Assembly Polls in 2020, National Democratic Alliance won 125 of the 243 seats and formed the government under the leadership of Nitish Kumar. Tejashwi Yadav, became the leader of opposition as well as of the Mahagatbandhan alliance which won 110 seats. He was short of majority by 12 seats. Lalu, embattled by legal cases and poor health, has been in and out of jail since his first incarceration in a fodder scam in 1997. Soon after an arrest warrant was issued against him, he had handed over charge as chief minister to Rabri Devi in July 1997 inviting huge criticism from all quarters. Rabri, till then just a wife and mother, a political nobody, ruled the state till 2005.

Tejashwi was a professional cricketer who played matches as late as 2010 but had gradually started taking interest in politics. He finally quit his passion for cricket in 2013 and entered the rough and tumble of politics as assembly elections were due in 2015, which was contested by RJD in alliance with the JD(U). Apparently, it was Tejashwi who had master-minded the alliance with the JD(U), which paid rich dividends in the polls. Prashant Kishor, who is now a competitor, had strategised their win.

Tejashwi became deputy CM under Nitish Kumar but the government did not complete its full five-year term. The unpredictable Nitish Kumar snapped ties with the RJD after CBI registered a corruption case against the Yadav family.

However, to ensure he continued on the CM's chair, Nitish joined hands with the BJP. Tejashwi became the leader of the opposition. Soon he became the face of the RJD in Bihar.

All eyes are now on the 2025 State Assembly elections to be held in October or November. Lalu wants to see Tejashwi on the CM's chair before he declares him the national president of RJD.

His siblings want power and would remain silent till 2025. Swords would be out if Tejashwi fails to deliver and then Lalu will have to do crisis management at home.

Mulayam and Lalu are relatives, but the former proved to be wiser than the latter. Once asked if he would like to declare his successor during his lifetime, Mulayam had quipped, 'Why should I bother what happens after me.' Lalu was one among many others who had told him to give this a serious thought.

Lalu may still be writing the dramatic end—only if he has a script! Why do leaders, who neither hail from political families nor support promotion of family members in politics finally fall for their children? The reasons can be other than the love for your kin.

Obviously, a son or daughter becomes a unifying force in a party with many aspirants—the cadres accept them unequivocally.

Second, in an era of *Aya Rams* and *Gaya Rams*, the paternal head of the party would like to hand it over to trusted hands, who would not close shop under any circumstances or for greed. Bigger fish always like to swallow the smaller fish—in politics, it's called merger.

Chapter 4

Succession

In the Hands of the People

Ironically, regional satraps have either promoted their progenies or none, as over the years, family members were accepted as natural claimants of their legacies across regions.

The BJP had incessantly waged a war against the Gandhi family for brazenly heading the Congress for half a century till eighty-two-year-old Mallikarjun Kharge was elected president in 2022.

However, dynastic politics could never become a viable issue in the elections as the voters largely wanted a leader of their choice, whether a dynast or a non-dynast. Unequivocally, Rahul Gandhi, the Congress scion, was not rejected by the voters in 2014, 2019 and 2024 General Elections, because he was a dynast who monopolised power. It's just that the voters found Narendra Modi more qualified for the Prime Minister's position.

Academically, dynastic politics is a subject of discussion as it does stifle competition in an uneven playing field. However, this is also a hard truth that the title or the surname has helped the heirs in acquiring a ready political base and quick acceptability by the cadres as well as the voters.

Thus, political dynasties have not only become a big reality but are also flourishing across several countries. However, while some ageing patriarchs have successfully scripted their succession plan, some decided to leave the decision to the public, either due to their own insecurities or indecisiveness.

Even corporate houses or small businesses evolve succession plans, primarily for the stability of their companies.

Political expert Varghese K George, however, is of the view that the succession battles were inevitable even after the declaration of a legal heir. He quoted the example of Shiv Sena, which had suffered an ugly split even after the party's giant Bal Thackeray had anointed his son Uddhav Thackeray as his rightful heir. His nephew Raj Thackeray had not only rebelled against the decision and quit the party, but had also floated a parallel outfit, the Maharashtra Navnirman Sena (MNS) whose political relevance is now limited to hurting his uncle's party in the elections. Raj Thackeray had failed to get even his son Amit Thackeray elected in his poll debut in 2024.

Nonetheless, the future of parties with no succession plan or heir apparent are also in doldrums, like Biju Janata Dal (BJD) in Odisha, Janata Dal U (JDU) in Bihar and AIADMK in Tamil Nadu, to name a few.

The BJD owed its humiliating defeat in the 2024 Assembly and Lok Sabha elections to the confusion over the succession issue, besides the voter's quest for a change in leadership.

BJD's popular leader Naveen Patnaik's decision against a succession plan or a successor was in everyone's knowledge. However, it was his failure to effectively counter the BJP's canard about his purported successor, a Tamilian and an outsider, that actually had a cascading effect on his electoral prospects.

During the 2024 General Elections when Prime Minister Narendra Modi had made a mischievous statement, 'I don't have any successor, people of this country are my successors,' he had known that the BJP's ideological parent, the RSS would take a call on the contentious issue of his successor at the right time, which could be 2025 when he would turn 75 years. The discussions about his successor have already begun.

As BJP is a cadre-based party, it would remain stable despite names of several aspirants in discussions. They would accept the leader hoisted on them as they have grown in a different culture and structure. Some inconsequential spurts of anger would not impact the huge party's overall health. The successor and succession have different connotations.

Thus, when Naveen Patnaik had said that the people of Odisha would decide his successor, they actually saw a vacuum and bleak future of the BJD, as he had not evolved any system to select or elect his heir. A successor is chosen, while succession is transferred.

After the demise of his father, a political stalwart Biju Patnaik, in 1997, an apolitical Naveen had taken the plunge to serve the state even though he had known little about its language and culture. Today, there is none in his family, who would come forward to take up the responsibility of the BJD. Naveen could have looked beyond his family to find his successor.

Naveen had lived abroad and had little interest in politics till the death of his father Biju Patnaik, who throughout his life remained on an adventurous mission.

As a pilot, Biju along with his pilot wife Gyan, had contributed immensely to India's freedom struggle, caring little about their own well-being. He had entered politics in 1946 and had never looked back again till his death in April 1997. In the rarest of the rare cases in Indian politics, Biju was elected unopposed to the Odisha State Assembly from North Cuttack constituency. The opposition had not filed any candidate against him.

A former union minister, two-time chief minister, he had worked closely with a galaxy of leaders, including Jawaharlal Nehru and Indira Gandhi. After quitting the Congress, he had become a key player in Janata Dal and Janata Party. In his later years, he was close to Vajpayee.

Naveen Patnaik, on the other hand, was a socialite, who at one time had rubbed shoulders with Delhi's glitterati at high profile dinners before he had embraced socialism. He was an author, who penned four books and innumerable articles on culture, art and social development. He had also acted in a Hollywood movie, *The Deceivers*, directed by Nicholas Meyer, which was released in 1988. All through, while he was chasing his varied passions, he had perhaps never realised that politics was in his blood.

John Elliott writes:

> I remember Naveen Patnaik talking emotionally at Delhi dinner parties of how ineffectual he felt (and was) in the face of the state's appalling rural poverty, which he was personally encountering for the first time. He later became the state's semi-reclusive chief minister and astounded both supporters and critics by being elected consecutively three times. (John Elliott, in his book *Implosion*, page 199, published by Harper Collins)

On his legacy, John writes:

> He has never married, so has no heirs to succeed him. Perhaps conscious that a rival Patnaik family had lost elections because voters had tired of their dynasty, he has played down his own family links and his brother and sister are rarely seen in Odisha. So, unless one of them changes their mind and decides to cash in on the family legacy, Naveen might close the dynasty, at least for a time.

Many in the past had described Naveen's entry into the unknown and untested territory of politics 'accidental' and 'unplanned,' but he must have had a political instinct to return and rule the state he had known little about and become a successful politician, a Machiavellian par excellence at the age of 50 years.

I asked Rajesh Mahapatra about Naveen's decision to enter politics. The Founder Director of Odisha Dialogues, an Odisha-focussed thought leadership forum, said, 'Yes, Naveen had hardly spent any time in Odisha before he entered public life following his father's death. Nor did he speak Odia. But in a very short time, he had come to understand Odisha and the Odia people much better than most politicians of Odisha.'

Naveen's entry into politics was unexpected. It was driven by circumstances, which had eventually marked a major turning point in Odisha politics, Mahapatra said.

After Biju's death in April 1997, senior Janata Dal leaders had feared a split in the party's rudderless state unit, as its members were being wooed by both the Congress party, which was then in power in Odisha, and a resurgent BJP that was aggressively trying to expand its footprint in the eastern state.

Around the same time, the Janata Dal was also facing a crisis at the national level, following a change of guard at the Centre—Inder Kumar Gujral had replaced HD Deve Gowda as the Prime Minister of the Janata Dal-led United Front government in New Delhi.

Biju's close associates had then rushed to his New Delhi home at 2, Aurangzeb Road, to persuade his eldest son Prem Patnaik to take charge of the party unit in Odisha. Prem, a businessman, had declined the offer and is believed to have said, 'I have no interest. Pappu (Naveen's nickname) *ko le jao*.' Naveen was also present at the meeting and had reluctantly agreed to take charge, following which the Odisha unit of Janata Dal split from the parent party and the Biju Janata Dal was born.

According to another version, the former BJP Prime Minister Atal Bihari Vajpayee, who was close to Biju Patnaik along with LK Advani had encouraged Naveen to step into his father's shoes, as they too had realised that the BJP had no presence in the state and only a strong regional leader could checkmate the Congress.

How different the approach of BJP leaders was then as compared to now!

Their plan had paid off as till date the Congress continues to struggle, while the BJP finally won Odisha in 2024, almost three decades after missing their first opportunity.

Many who had believed that Naveen did not have any grain of politics in his veins were proved wrong, as he became the longest serving CM of the country (2000-2024) after Pawan Kumar Chamling of Sikkim. Naveen would have broken Chamling's record if he had won the 2024 Assembly elections. It's all because of his acumen and judicious decisions that his regional party could control the politics of the state keeping national parties out of its boundaries.

The pace and the rise of the leader who had surprised all by his political accomplishments, Naveen had formed the BJD in December 1997 within months of his father's demise in April. His fledgling party won nine Lok Sabha seats in the 1998 General Elections. He started his political career as Union Minister of State for Mines. Odisha has twenty-one Lok Sabha seats.

In the subsequent elections in 1999 and 2004, the BJD had increased its tally by one seat each—ten and eleven in the Lok Sabha. The party had won a majority in the State Assembly elections in alliance with the BJP in 2000 and 2004 and formed the state government. However, after the Kandhamal communal riots of 2008, the BJD had snapped ties with the BJP.

The riots had rocked Kandhamal district after the murder of a Hindu monk Lakshmananda Saraswati in which thirty-nine Christians had lost their lives, while thousands were displaced and several churches were burnt by some Hindu organisations.

Despite the gruesome incident in his state that had led to the collapse of his alliance with the BJP, Naveen had managed to increase his tally in the Lok Sabha elections to fourteen in 2009 and twenty in 2014, when the Narendra Modi wave was sweeping the rest of the country. BJD's tally in the Lok Sabha had dipped to twelve in 2019 followed with a complete rout in 2024. The BJP had won twenty seats and Congress one. It was BJD's first defeat since Naveen's debut in politics.

Though the people of Odisha claim to live by their popular catchphrase, '*Odisara Neta Nahin Prayojam, Odisara Neta Swayam Narain* (Odisha does not need a leader, we have leader in Jagannath), yet in 2024 they were swept by Narendra Modi's aura and a strong desire for a change of leadership. Such was the influence of Modi on them that they had even ignored the unpalatable statement of the BJP's spokesman Sambit Patra, 'Jagannath is Modi *Bhakt*.'

The BJD was born on the slogan of *Odia Asmita* (Proud Odia) and it lost the state on the same slogan in 2024, as Naveen had failed to counter the BJP's propaganda about an 'outsider' controlling Naveen and their Odisha.

The BJP, led by Modi, an old-time friend of Naveen Patnaik, and Home Minister Amit Shah had built an aggressive and an acrimonious campaign against him on two issues. One, the influence of ex-bureaucrat VK Pandian, who hailed from Tamil Nadu, on their CM. Amit Shah had openly asked the voters, 'Should Odisha be run by Tamil Babu. Naveen Babu is unwell, he does not run his government, a Tamil Babu runs it.' The BJP had also written a letter to the state police chief alleging the CM had been kept hostage by Pandian and some non-Odia officers.

The Odisha CM did try his best to dispel the misconception that VK Pandian was his successor. He had repeatedly clarified that the public and the party would choose the leader to inherit his legacy. However, his explanations failed to stem the tide against him as the public was upset by the huge hoardings of Pandian dwarfing Patnaik. The BJP robbed the BJD of its emotive *Odia Asmita* (the pride of being an Odia) slogan.

Odisha has always preferred their regional player in Biju Patnaik and his son Naveen Patnaik, who also used to play up their regional credentials. On every foundation day of the BJD, Naveen used to tom-tom the party's regional agenda saying, 'Every other political party goes to Delhi to get instructions while we decide our fate here.'

It's not that he did not have a tacit understanding with the Centre, but it was on clear terms, 'You rule Delhi, I rule here.' Like his father he had also epitomised Odia pride. But in 2024, a babu from the south had deflated it.

Naveen's age and ill-health was the second issue that was projected against him with the Prime Minister promising to give a young leader to the state. Though Naveen had actually slowed down with age, he had strongly rebutted it with his social media team releasing videos of his campaigning across the state to dispel public doubts about his health.

Naveen had also refuted his poor health campaign at a public meeting, ridiculing the PM for instituting an inquiry into his fragile health. 'If he was actually concerned about my health, all that Modi had to do was to pick up a phone and call.'

A student, who drove a cab to make some extra pocket money

in Pune, was candid enough to attribute Patnaik's defeat to his age and their desire for a new young leadership, which the BJP had promised.

The BJD leaders were confident their mass leader Naveen Patnaik would break Sikkim's record of giving the longest serving CM to the country by winning the 2024 assembly polls. They were less bothered about the BJP winning the Lok Sabha polls as their interest was in protecting their own turf.

People wanted change and stability, and somehow the BJD headed by a seventy-seven-year-old popular leader, with no successor in sight except for an outsider, VK Pandian, failed to convince or impress them.

Is it the end of the road for the BJD?

Rajesh Mahapatra says it's too early to draw any conclusion about the party's future before getting answers to some knotty questions.

'Was the unexpected defeat of the BJD a manifestation of anti-Pandian sentiments only? Or is it also a reflection of the voters in Odisha shedding their preference for a regional party in favour of a national party? Will regional identity continue to influence electoral outcomes as it has done in the past or is the game over for now? Despite the loss in the 2024 elections, Naveen remains the most popular figure in Odisha. How will he play the politics of opposition now?

The answers to these questions would decide the politics of tomorrow in Odisha, Mahapatra said. A survey is on!

Naveen has graciously exited from power, but would he want the party's exit from Odisha's political map? If not, then the people want him to decide his legacy. He is right now playing the role of a constructive opposition leader, telling the workers not to be ashamed of loss but take pride in the work done by the government. But the pertinent question before the people is who would lead the BJD in the next polls, five years later when Naveen would be eighty-two years old.

All along, Naveen's detractors had accused him of playing politics of self-preservation by systematically removing as many as fifty strong leaders from the party in the twenty-five years of his politics and thus smartly nipping rebellion in the bud. Even today, the party is said to be under the influence of a few leaders, who don't have their roots in BJD. His well-wishers feel the time had come for Naveen to take harsh decisions, if he actually wanted to preserve the party instead of himself or his close acolytes. His innings may be getting over, but the party is flush with funds and leadership, the two ingredients for survival.

Many of his admirers still believe that their leader Naveen Patnaik would bounce back as he has a sharp mind, to reaffirm which, they often quote an incident from his political diary. It's about Bijoy Mohapatra, a veteran, who could not enter the state assembly for twenty-four years after he was shown the door by Naveen. Mohapatra had contested elections several times as an independent, but Naveen ensured his defeat. Eventually his son joined the BJD and won assembly elections in 2024.

Political observers want to wait and watch till the 2027 Panchayat elections before writing off the BJD from the state's map as Naveen Babu may be working on a plan to oust the BJP from Odisha. The reversals in Panchayat elections would not upset the applecart, but actually galvanise, and not demoralise Naveen as well as his anti-forces in the party to save the BJD from division or death. The role of seniors would be crucial.

In 1997, when the party had faced a void after Biju's death, it had a number of committed leaders who had grown with him or were groomed by him. Still, when the time came for Biju's legacy, they had to depend on a family member and Naveen emerged as a saviour. Now there are no doors that they can knock on. His brother Prem's son is not interested in politics, while Naveen has neither married nor groomed his successor.

Would Naveen spring a surprise and foster a successful transition plan to save the party he raised as a much younger man? Some are pinning their hopes on his penchant for throwing surprises!

***

A story from the south

She saw the party dying but failed to decide her successor.

Maruthur Gopalan Ramachandran, popularly known as MGR, founder and first general secretary of AIADMK had encouraged his screen co-star J Jayalalithaa (born 1948) to join politics. She had a meteoric rise in the party hierarchy as she was erudite and proficient. Besides, she had the most vital ingredient for success in politics—the valuable backing of the party's leader, MGR.

Political observer Varghese K George says that Jayalalithaa was an undeclared but a clear successor of MGR. She had herself created this perception, but was side-lined after his death.

The party had briefly split into two factions after her haters had propped up MGR's wife VN Janaki, also an actor and activist, who was widely respected as MGR's wife. She became CM, lost a trust vote and quit politics forever. She remained MGR's wife and not his political successor. It was Jayalalithaa, who finally succeeded him and ruled the state for fourteen years over six terms—the first time in 1991.

Jayalalithaa had seen the party in disarray after MGR's death, yet she followed her mentor's footsteps and did not announce her political heirship during her lifetime. Perhaps, as written often in the media, she never wanted the party to survive after her. When MGR died, his fans had cried, 'Why should Madras survive when MGR was no more?' So, going by the same logic, why should AIADMK survive when she was not around?

The consequences of Jayalalithaa leaving AIADMK rudderless were huge—the party suffered and is struggling till date to regain its prime position it lost along with her demise in 2016.

AIADMK had won the 2016 assembly elections in May, and she passed away in December 2016. The party ruled the state till 2021 with change of leadership. O Panneerselvam (OPS) ruled for seventy-two days and Edappadi K Palaniswami (EPS) for four years and seventy-nine days.

Meanwhile, the rival DMK consolidated its position and is ruling the state since 2021. The AIADMK, locked in a war over leadership, has not tasted electoral success after the 2016 assembly elections.

The BJP, which had been trying to cultivate its political space in Tamil Nadu since 1998 found the going easier in AIADMK's absence. This was clearly reflected in the BJP's vote share, which jumped from 5 per cent in 2019 to 11.24 per cent in 2024, though it could not even win one seat.

The CSDS-Lokniti in its report, published in the media, did point out slight erosion in the bi-polarity of the state, leading to gains by the BJP.

Of the two regional players, the DMK stole the show in alliance with the Congress while the AIADMK lost all seats, forfeiting deposits on some. But its vote share remained intact—it had polled 19.39 per cent in 2019 and 20.46 per cent in 2024—a slight edge.

The results have come as a morale booster for the current leadership of AIADMK, under Palaniswami, to infuse life in the party before the next assembly elections in 2026. He has also given an ideological twist to the battle, declaring his determination to keep the Hindi speaking saffron power at bay. But in early 2025, he flew to Delhi and shook hands with the Union Home Minister Amit Shah triggering speculations about a possible alliance between the BJP and AIADMK in 2026. After all, the BJP will need a strong regional party as an ally to upstage the DMK.

OPS and EPS, as they are popularly known, have split after the 2021 State Assembly Elections. OPS, was thrown out of AIADMK in July 2022.

Kavitha Muralidharan wrote a brilliant piece on the tremors that Jayalalithaa's death had created in Tamil Nadu one year after her death. She wrote:

> They say nature abhors a vacuum and in the vacuum that she left behind, Tamil Nadu has witnessed many things that would have never happened if Amma was still alive. (*Hindustan Times*, 5 December 2017)

Kavitha mentioned about Jayalalithaa's soul sister Sasikala, whose clout people witnessed as she appointed OPS as CM in less than twelve hours after Jayalalithaa's death and later, on December 31, she officially took over as AIADMK's general secretary. The report in the *Hindustan Times* also mentions the following:

> There are two things that Jayalalithaa held very close as the party's basic tenets. The party was avowedly anti-DMK and it never encouraged family rule. Jayalalithaa had a visceral hatred for the DMK. But Sasikala and Dinakaran threw both to the winds. They have a tacit understanding with the DMK and by

appointing Dinakaran as the party's deputy general secretary, Sasikala betrayed Amma.

OPS had revolted against Sasikala in 2017 and was later expelled from the party. He is now fighting a lonely legal and political battle. However, the only solace for him was the dais he shared with the BJP during elections in 2024. Now the party is in full control of EPS and the BJP has no qualms in courting him.

AIADMK has been written off several times in the past, but then the party was led by charismatic leaders like MGR and Jayalalithaa. EPS does not come from the world of cinema but is a hardcore politician. The public will decide Jayalalithaa's successor as well as the party's fate in the 2026 Assembly polls.

***

West Bengal's succession story

The succession issue haunts West Bengal, too. The undisputed iron lady Mamata Banerjee has not yet officially declared her nephew Abhishek Banerjee as her legal heir, though it is again a kind of open secret.

Perhaps it's a tough call for Mamata Didi as she struggles against the BJP and would not want to ruffle feathers in her own party at this critical juncture. Any differences in TMC would work to her disadvantage.

The feisty leader of a robust TMC had fought male dominance in the Congress, had decimated and shut the shop of conservative Communists by ending the Left Front's uninterrupted thirty-four-year-old rule. She is currently engaged in a fierce fight with the BJP, but she fears announcing her heir apparent.

How come she lacks the guts to instal Abhishek Banerjee, her only relative in the party, as her successor?

While campaigning in Abhishek Banerjee's Lok Sabha constituency in Diamond Harbour, Mamata had fondly said, 'Abhishek has been in politics since he was two years old when CPM goons had attacked me. He saw me and shouted slogans seeking answers from CPM for attacking me.'

Was she addressing her senior party colleagues who are neither averse nor do they favour his immediate anointment?

TMC was formed in 1998 and she has been a majority CM since 2011. The party had completed twenty-five years in 2023 and she completed twenty-three years as CM.

The age of seventy is considered young in the profession of politics, and she is fighting fit with no physical ailments. She can walk miles and work endlessly.

She has been grooming her nephew as her legal heir. Abhishek had become a major player after her most trusted leader Mukul Roy, who knew how to hit and hurt her, defected to the BJP in 2017.

Earlier many senior leaders were not comfortable with the idea of Abhishek contesting Lok Sabha elections at the age of 26 in 2014.

> A fluent speaker, Abhishek Banerjee has imbibed his aunt's aggression and confidence, but as he made his political debut when Mamata Banerjee was in power, he lacks the baptism through the fire like his aunt, who survived decades of Left aggression in West Bengal. (Avijit Ghoshal, *Hindustan Times*, 15 April 2019)

In the same report, Ghoshal continues:

For Mamata Banerjee's political opponents, especially the Bharatiya Janata Party, Abhishek is a constant target. They think the easiest way of cornering Mamata Banerjee is by getting at Abhishek. No public speech of BJP leaders in the state is complete without a reference to "the nephew" and mention of disproportionate growth of his business and assets. But inquiries against him have not crystallised into any investigation so far. He has become the second most important campaigner in the Lok Sabha elections after Mamata Banerjee. However, he takes care never to refer to his relationship with the party chief and describes her as "our leader".

According to political observer Joyjit Ghosh, Mamata's actions and appointments speak volumes about Abhishek Banerjee's role and clout in the party. The heir apparent is the national general secretary and second in command in the organisation, which however is not very structured, as there are selections and not elections.

Thus, after the transition of the party's leadership from Mamata to Abhishek, the TMC will change from a one-woman-party to a one-man-party. While she is famous for her cotton sarees and slippers, the youth follow Abhishek's hairstyle, spectacles and white kurta pyjama.

However, some generational differences exist between the aunt and her nephew. While the former relies heavily on the old guards, who have been with the TMC since 1998, Abhishek Banerjee wants a retirement age in the party.

Abhishek has started grooming the younger crop and his loyalists have been demanding a bigger role or control for him, on the lines of Bihar and Uttar Pradesh. Joyjit doesn't foresee Abhishek becoming CM even after 2026 Assembly elections as Mamata is still young and not yet ready to relinquish active public life.

Nonetheless, the three-term MP would still find it tough to take complete control of TMC in case Mamata fails to settle him in the coveted chair during her lifetime. The BJP has been baying for her blood and after its spectacular win in Odisha in 2024, West Bengal is high on their agenda. The voters will accept Abhishek, but other claimants could always arise, sometimes prompted by competitors. The scene is similar to Bihar with three interesting political features.

JD(U) President Nitish Kumar has been CM since February 2015, though his party had never won a majority on its own.

Nitish has never ever compromised on the CM's position, (he previously held office from 2005-2014 and for a short period in 2000) while the supporting partners or allies kept changing—from NDA to Mahagatbandhan and again, to NDA. He smiles when he is dubbed as '*Paltu* Ram' (turncoat) or in the words of RJD leader Tejashwi Yadav, '*Aisa koi dal nahin jisko chacha* (Nitish Kumar) *ne thaga nahin*. (There is no party whom uncle has not betrayed.)'

The JD(U) President is credited for never promoting his family members in politics or engaging in corrupt tactics. Prime Minister Narendra Modi recently described him as Bihar's '*ladle* CM'(adorable CM).

In 2005 and 2010, Nitish Kumar had headed a JD(U)-NDA coalition government. However, in 2013 he had snapped ties with the BJP in protest against the party's decision to declare the then Gujarat CM Narendra Modi as their Prime Ministerial candidate. He had then formed a Grand Alliance with the RJD and the Congress. He had quit office on moral grounds after JD(U) lost the 2014 Lok Sabha polls and had chosen Jitan Ram Manjhi as his replacement. Manjhi later formed his own party, Hindustani Awam Morcha, after his expulsion from JD(U) over a leadership tussle in 2015. Manjhi is a minister in the Modi government at the Centre.

In 2017, Nitish had again broken ties with the RJD following Lalu Yadav's implication in the Fodder Scam and returned to the NDA, which was re-elected in the 2020 Assembly Polls. In August 2022, Nitish quit the NDA and joined the Grand Alliance, only to re-join NDA in January 2024.

A very convoluted journey!

JD(U) is now one of the two crutches on which the Narendra Modi government survives.

Nitish Kumar is seventy-nine years old and not in the best of health, but he has not yet announced his successor. Ask anyone—from politicians to political observers—about the future of the JD(U), and the answer is the same. In unison, they will say, 'It's written on the wall—the party will be finished.'

Ajay Kumar of *Bihar Times* holds the same view, 'The party has no successor, no structure, no ideological bearing—obviously the workers are demoralised, disillusioned knowing the gloomy fate of JD(U) for which they had slogged and struggled.'

Political expert Mukesh Kumar says, 'JD(U)is alive till Nitish is around. It would split with a big chunk going to the BJP.'

Shambhu Sharan Srivastava, who has been associated with Nitish was candid in admitting that the JD(U) had no future, no stake after Nitish was not around. The party would be up for grabs. And the BJP would be the first to strike.

According to him it was still not too late to announce a successor, though many names are being discussed, but Nitish's blessings would make it easier for his successor to settle. However, people would only accept Kurmi leadership.

Interestingly, of the three dominant OBCs (other backward castes) in Bihar— Kurmi, Yadav and Kushwaha—the core voters of the JD(U) are Kurmis, who have grown big in education, jobs and business; and they may now prefer a national party. However, their first choice would be a Kurmi leader and they can persuade or pressurise Nitish to announce his successor.

In early 2025, his engineer son Nishant Kumar came out of the shadows and demanded that both the NDA and JD(U) should declare his father as the CM. He interacted with the media as well as party workers to propagate the exemplary work done by his father during his nineteen-year-long rule in the state.

Nishant stepped in at the time when some key leaders of the party had started hobnobbing with the BJP leadership believing it was time out for Nitish Kumar. Nishant put to rest all speculations about his father's health but remained evasive on joining politics. Nitish, who has been vociferously against dynastic politics, would find it hard to declare Nishant his successor and his son's political entry would need his approval. The picture would be clearer in the future as the BJP is desperate to crack the second most crucial state of Northern India and they cannot accomplish their dream project without the support of Nitish Kumar. The only leader acceptable to the powerful Kurmis, the backbone of JD(U), would be Nishant after Nitish. Or else the party could disintegrate along with its vote bank.

JD(U) is a splinter group of the Janata Dal. It was formed by the merger of the Sharad Yadav faction of JD, the Lok Shakti and Samata Party in 2003. Nitish's importance lies in his image of a gentleman like Naveen Patnaik. Both are brilliant, but the Bihari Babu is distinctly unpredictable.

Nitish has always been in demand, both by the BJP as well as RJD, as he tilts the scales in the favour of the party he allies with in the elections. Interestingly, all eyes even today are on him. What if he makes a volte face?

In any way, he cares little if JD(U) divides and dies in the process.

Chapter 5

Three Women Satraps Men Feared!

'Well, a Clinton can win, not Hillary,' said an American journalist during discussions on the presidential elections in one of the world's largest democracies, the United States of America. His demeaning comment on the electoral prospects of Hillary Rodham Clinton had caught me off guard. She had announced her candidacy for president, but had eventually lost in the Democratic Primary to Obama in the 2008 presidential polls.

'It's a sexist comment,' I quietly said. He smiled and replied, 'Women here don't make it to the top of the organisations, even if it is political.' Why? The answer was equally abhorrent: 'Maybe people are distrustful of women candidates and their capabilities!' Clinton later in 2016 became the first woman in history to represent a major party in a presidential election.

In 2008 when Clinton was facing rejection primarily because she was a woman, here in India, a Dalit woman Chief Minister Mayawati was running the country's largest state of Uttar Pradesh. The same year, Sheila Dikshit had become CM of Delhi, the country's capital for the second term.

India, another large democracy in the world, had its first

woman Prime Minister Indira Gandhi, fifty-eight years back in 1966. Since then, women have occupied coveted positions of President, Speaker of the Lok Sabha, Chief Minister, Governor, and Cabinet Ministers, to mention a few.

Yet their strength in the state legislatures and Parliament, since the time they had graced the first meeting of the Constituent Assembly on 6 December 1946 at the Constitution Hall in New Delhi's Rafi Marg, has been dismal.

The problem here lies with the political parties and their patriarchal structure that discourages women in leadership roles, especially the ones coming from an apolitical background.

Of the seven national parties, Congress is the only party which has been thrice headed by a woman President—twice for familial reasons. As daughter of Congress President and the country's first Prime Minister Jawaharlal Nehru, Indira Gandhi had become the Congress President in 1959, while her daughter-in-law and a reluctant politician Sonia Gandhi inherited the coveted position in 1998 to ultimately become the longest serving president of the party.

Despite a discouraging political environment, three women from a non-political background and varied castes had taken a plunge into the rough and tumble of politics in three different corners of the country—North-East, North and South—and emerged as the undisputed commanders of their outfits. They headed regional parties, formed by them or their mentors.

Mamata Banerjee, a Brahmin in West Bengal, J Jayalalithaa, a Brahmin in Tamil Nadu and Mayawati, a Jatav (Scheduled Caste) in Uttar Pradesh had to literally sweat it out before they were accepted as leaders of repute.

Mamata was the daughter of a Congress worker who passed away when she was only seventeen years old. She had joined the students' union of Jogamaya Devi College to relive her father's dreams. By her sheer diligence and hard work, Mamata got elected as the general secretary of the women's wing of the Congress in West Bengal.

Politics of many women leaders end at this level as their male counterparts simply cannot envision them holding decision-making senior positions in the political set-up dominated by them.

Mamata was made of a different mettle and has risen through the ranks, bravely pushing away hecklers and overcoming roadblocks. She had first come into the limelight after defeating the CPM giant Somnath Chatterjee in the 1984 assembly elections to emerge as the youngest MP at thirty-one.

Let's turn to the South: Jayalalithaa was pushed into cinema at a young age by her mother, a theatre artist, who used to play small roles in films to feed her family. Jayalalithaa was a trained dancer and had taken lessons in classical music and western classical music and had reluctantly started working in films where she met MG Ramachandran and was inspired by his politics.

Jayalalithaa, who firmly believed that she was cut out for politics, soon started working on her dreams. She was already a popular star, who wanted to shine in the political world instead of Tollywood.

She was groomed by her co-star, MG Ramachandran, a superstar and a political icon, who founded the AIADMK in 1972 after his expulsion from the DMK.

Now, let us move to the caste-conscious North India in the largest state of the country. Mayawati, a Jatav, was daughter of a post office employee who lived in the Patparganj area of New Delhi. She faced gender inequality at home and caste discrimination in society. While her brothers studied in public schools, Mayawati was sent to a *Sarkari Vidyalaya* (government school). Yet, she completed Law and B.Ed. She had started teaching in a school while simultaneously preparing for the civil services exams when Kanshi Ram spotted her at one of his functions. Bowled over by her fiery speech, he invited her to join his mission to unite the Bahujan Samaj in the country. And for this, he visited her home.

While Mamata had to fight and fend for herself, Mayawati and Jayalalithaa had the blessings and backing of their mentors—Kanshi Ram and MGR respectively—the men behind the success of these two women icons.

The three women leaders—Mayawati, Jayalalithaa and Mamata—had faced stiff opposition from their male colleagues as they detested their phoenix-like rise in the party, but the trio did not shudder or stop. They were pulled down, physically assaulted and humiliated, but the three gutsy women fought and found their way to the top of the ladder.

Mamata Banerjee had taken her first political lessons in the grand old party, the Congress, which was then plagued by internecine squabbles. She ruthlessly split from her alma mater and founded Trinamool Congress in 1997.

> In the first phase of her political career, Banerjee fought against the overwhelmingly male dominion within the Congress. Then she fought the paternalism that prevented her ambitious bid to take over the leadership of the West Bengal Congress, and forced her to break away and form her own political party. (*Mamata: Beyond 2021* by Jayanta Ghoshal, translated from Bengali by Arunava Sinha)

Jayalalithaa struggled for two years after the demise of MGR in 1987 to take over AIADMK. His death had vertically split the party into two factions with a section of the leaders demanding that MGR's wife VN Janaki Ramachandran take over his position.

Even though she was not active in politics, she relented before their wishes. The Congress was also supporting her and she became the first woman film star to grace the coveted chair of the Tamil Nadu Chief Minister. She, however, lost the vote of confidence in the State Assembly. After splits and slander, Jayalalithaa unified the party and became its undisputed leader in 1989.

Similarly, in Uttar Pradesh, the co-founders of the Dalit movement had strongly opposed founder Kanshi Ram's plan to instal Mayawati as head of the BSP. Their association with him had been long as they had together founded the All India Backward and Minority Community Employees Cooperative Federation (BAMCEF) in 1971 and Dalit Shoshit Samaj Sangharsh Samiti in 1981. The BSP was formed in 1984.

Mayawati was in her twenties when she joined Kanshi Ram's bandwagon. Her quick promotion in the party triggered off an exodus by senior leaders. Amid street fights, claims and counter claims, Kanshi Ram announced Mayawati as his successor in December 2001. She became President of the BSP in September 2003. Several splinter groups of BSP cropped up across the state.

Both Jayalalithaa and Mayawati had to face character assassination at every step. Instead of shedding tears at home, they hit back at those who accused them of rising swiftly in the party hierarchy because of their illicit relations with their political gurus. Simultaneously, they did not have any inhibitions in flaunting their closeness with their mentors.

> Jayalalithaa often said: Our relationship is very peculiar. Although he is so much older than me, every spare moment on the film sets, we would spend talking to each other, discussing every subject under the sun. We used to talk about science, philosophy, literature. Both of us are deeply interested in classical music, astrology and astronomy. We have so much in

common. (Vaasanthi, *Amma: Jayalalithaa's Journey from Movie Star to Political Queen*, excerpts of which were published by *Mint*, 6 December 2017)

Jayalalithaa did not mince words in saying, 'He is everything to me. He is my father, mother, mentor, friend, philosopher and guide. He is my anchor. He will never let me down. He never lets down anyone who believes in him.' Of course, she did not ever say 'he is also my lover,' but the party cadres thought he was and that made her more special and lovable to them. She gave the impression that her mandate from MGR was absolute, wrote Vaasanthi.

Mayawati had also silenced her detractors saying, 'He is my guru. He is elder to me in age. I have his blessings. Both of us had to struggle hard as we did not get politics as a legacy. In his sickness, people say that a son can't take care of his father as much as I am doing.' She had also said the same thing to me.

Mayawati loved and accepted challenges. She courted controversies. Unfazed by the uproar her actions evoked, she often walked the road that others like her would avoid like the plague. She often said, 'I have transformed myself into a rock that does not melt but turns the course of rivers.'

Both Jayalalithaa and Mayawati were confident that once their solitary trek on thorns would end on the throne, the same men would shamelessly play subservient, even lying prostate before them in full public glare.

And it actually did happen! Both broke the glass ceiling by heading their regional parties amid cries and protests and by becoming the first woman Chief Ministers of their states.

Both of them also shattered caste barriers. Jayalalithaa, transformed the face of the Dravidian movement which was formed on the principles of anti-Brahminism and Mayawati, as *Dalit ki Beti* broke the upper caste hegemony in Uttar Pradesh.

As Mamata had founded TMC, no questions could be raised on her presidentship. Still, it was not easy for her to demolish the deeply entrenched male-dominated Communist citadel and become West Bengal's first woman chief minister.

In the 2024 General Elections, when many thought Mamata would succumb and surrender to pressures from an aggressive and ambitious BJP, which was determined to capture her bastion, the Bengali tigress roared back. She single-handedly crushed them and their challenge, demolishing their dreams of hoisting their flag on her state and defied the obituaries that were written on her political life.

Ahead of the 2024 polls, Mamata had advocated that an opposition alliance could take on the mighty BJP in the country, but in her own state, she fought the war alone and won it with flying colours.

The three women regional satraps have thus created history of sorts giving their male counterparts strong competition.

But in the strenuous world and process of politics, Mamata, Mayawati and Jayalalithaa became both reclusive and ruthless. They detested perfidy, but rewarded loyalty. They loved sycophancy, but despised in-house conspiracies. They won elections for their parties, but demanded obsequiousness in return, tolerating no questions, and no arguments. They trusted none.

Were they born like that? Perhaps not, but they knew they would have to project a stronger exterior to survive in the male-dominated world of politics, as any softness in their demeanour would be misunderstood as political weakness. They actually proved to be the only strong personalities in their party and the cabinet.

The transformation

The proverb 'clothes make the man' is also an apt expression to describe women in leadership roles, especially in the political domain. Studies have shown that generally people judge others from the clothes they wear, even though this may be only a half-truth.

In a patriarchal or male chauvinistic society, the character and capacity of working women is judged more on the basis of their looks, dressing style, wardrobe, hair style and bags.

Indira Gandhi was discussed more for her cotton, well-starched sarees, bob-cut hairstyle and evocative eyes than for her stirring speeches and political acumen till she displayed the mettle she was made of in both her decisions and actions. Though she was the daughter of the country's first Prime Minister, Jawaharlal Nehru, she still suffered snide comments like '*goongi gudiya*' (dumb doll) till she displayed her iron fist.

Mamata, Mayawati and Jayalalithaa had no high-profile political families to pitchfork or protect them in the political sphere. Thus, their challenges were huge.

As the three regional satraps wrestled their way through the choppy waters, they were repeatedly tested for their political prowess, which they cleared with aplomb, while their feminine assets were discussed more with '*mirch* and *masala*' (spice). They wanted to be judged for their performance rather than their persona. Thus, Jayalalitha and Mayawati changed their dressing style as well as their lifestyle.

Prudently, the three strong women had carefully changed their public image. The TMC slogan of '*Bangla nijer meyekei chaye*' (Bengal wants its own daughter), endeared Mamata as 'Didi', so much so that the country's popular Prime Minister Narendra Modi paid a price for his taunt '*Didi oh Didi*' at his rallies in the 2019 Lok Sabha elections. Jaya became *amma* (mother) and Mayawati *behenji* (sister).

Jayalalithaa came from the glamour world and had a charismatic personality. Her major challenge was to transform her public image from a glam doll to a suave politician who meant business.

Tollywood has produced several politicians in South India including five Chief Ministers of the state—C N Annadurai, M Karunanidhi, MG Ramachandran, Janaki Ramachandran (briefly), and J Jayalalithaa.

Her mentor, MGR had intelligently appropriated his ideology in films by playing roles that helped in creating his political image. Others did the same. But Jayalalithaa did not have the choice to use the screen to build an image of Mother India for herself.

On the demand of her film directors, she played romantic roles, wore swimsuits and defended her choice of roles, saying that one could not wear a *salwar kameez* in a swimming pool. Her onscreen persona of a glam doll got her audience into auditoriums, but it was not helping her in fetching votes in the political world. She had to struggle to emerge out of her onscreen image of a glamorous romantic actress and be taken for a serious politician.

Offscreen, she started wearing plain sarees with a cape, with no accessories like jewellery or make up. She walked slowly, and spoke softly. However, she lived like a queen in her inaccessible Pose Garden mansion, where only Sasikala, her friend and confidante had access. It was only after the raid by income tax sleuths in 1996 that the world came to know about her ornate and ostentatious lifestyle.

What did she do with her 10,500 sarees, 750 pairs of slippers, 500 wine glasses, designer bags and kilos of gold and silver jewellery when she couldn't wear them in public? The haul, was displayed to the public, but it did not shrink her support base as her political trajectory reveals. She had been accepted as Amma by then.

Slowly, people who sometimes called MGR as *Anna* or elder brother, started calling Jayalalithaa *Anni*—wife of elder brother, but she steadily cultivated the image of a benevolent mother or Amma, who blessed her constituents, especially women with a chain of welfare schemes that touched their lives—from Amma canteen, Amma salt, Amma water bottles, and Amma maternity kits. Populism was the word to describe her style of politics.

Mayawati faced a different problem as she had come from a lower caste, Jatav, who even now are treated as untouchables in several parts of the country. But she used her status of *Dalit ki Beti* to her advantage—to change the mindsets of the people in a caste conscious society. She knew people would bow before power, irrespective of the caste they belonged to.

Initially Mayawati used to meet visitors and officers in a simple gown and this raised eyebrows. As she brooked no nonsense from anyone, her inner coterie lacked the courage to tell her about the gossip that her gowns were generating outside the Chief Minister's residence. The gowns, seen as nightwear, were not making a fashion statement.

One day, she was casually told to wear something formal as expected from the CM, the head of the state. An officer, who was present then, shared her innocent reply—'If you people so desire, I won't wear gowns.' However, she did not understand why she should not wear gowns that she often saw woman wearing on the streets in Patparganj.

Mayawati became the quintessential *behenji*. She loved jewellery especially diamonds that she flashed and flaunted on her birthdays. The sparkling diamonds became a symbol of empowerment for Dalit women. On working days, she would wear a dull beige suit and would don a suit of bright pink on special occasions. Many fashion designers vied to change her dressing style, but Mayawati had no time or interest in opting for a makeover.

Still, she became a style icon for her young followers in rural areas and many women sported the same hairstyle as hers till she had a haircut. Her ponytails with pompom hair ties became a craze in the countryside. They adored her and disbelieved sting operations that revealed the wealth she had amassed.

They instead believed every word Mayawati said to the media: 'How can I be blamed if some of my well-wishers gift me land or money? But *manuvadi* parties raise these issues to defame me in the Bahujan Samaj. As far as my parents or my relatives are concerned, how am I involved if they start their business from the money they have or borrow? Whatever I have is recorded with the Income Tax.'

Her every word was Gospel to her followers. Even if they saw certain videos, or CDs, they believed none of them.

Once when she had kicked off a controversy by accepting a garland of currency notes, her supporters had defended her by raising a counter question, 'What is wrong in accepting a garland of currency notes? She is not the first one? Leaders have been weighed in coins even in the past but no one reacted then. Why this hue and cry when the daughter of a Dalit has been offered a garland of currency notes?' Her big purse also always evoked much curiosity.

Mayawati, who often sounded dictatorial, sometimes came out as a simple woman who could talk about *pakoras* and *chutney*, cleanliness at home and in her office. She even explained her diktat to all officers—take off their shoes before entering her room as she was allergic to dust. Mayawati also clarified her decision to cut her hair short.

'I wanted to save time to serve the poor,' she had told me in a one-on-one informal chat, sometime in 2006, when she was more accessible to journalists.

So, while her political detractors dubbed her as a megalomaniac who brazenly accepted gold and silver crowns, garlands made of currency notes and costly birthday gifts, her defiant supporters countered it by gifting her crowns and cash.

People don't remember seeing Mamata ever in a flashy or classy saree. Instead, her trademark white saree with mono colour borders and slippers, hair roughly tied up, sometimes ruffled too, made a unique fashion statement.

She met high-profile diplomats, attended official dinners or weddings as CM in her cotton sarees. In 2017, when she had attended dinner at industrialist Mukesh Ambani's 27-storey home, *Antila*, to garner investments for her state, she was dressed in a simple white saree with a brown border, and the same colour of slippers. No one made any mention of what she wore, as her face was glowing with an inexplicable confidence.

Again, at Mukesh Ambani's daughter Isha Ambani's wedding, in December 2018, Mamata, the Bengal tigress had stood out in her *beguni* border *Dhaniakhali* saree, with flip flops rubbing shoulders with the glitterati in their designer clothes and sparking diamonds.

Mamata dazzled in her simplicity—that's the strength of power. Her handloom sarees are now labelled as 'Mamata sarees.'

'Courage and conviction are two words very easy to pronounce, but very difficult to practice. She is a lady who never wore lipstick, never wore a saree that cost more than Rs 500,'

Trinamool leader, Partha Chatterjee, who has been with Mamata since her college days had once said.

She continues to live in her ancestral terracotta tiled roof house at Harish Chandra Street in Kolkata even now.

Interestingly, her books, poetry and paintings are discussed more than what she wears and when.

Eventually, the focus in all the three states from where these three chief ministers hailed shifted from their appearance to their acumen to win poll battles. Their politics, however, left many injured or bruised.

Turning point

Unfortunately, the turning point in their lives was as dramatic as traumatic.

It was in 1989, when Mamata sustained life-threatening head injuries during a protest rally in Kolkata. She was general secretary of the All-India Youth Congress and was beaten up by CPM supporters. Having defeated Communist giant Somnath Chatterjee in the 1984 Lok Sabha elections, she had emerged as a force to reckon with and CPM leaders had felt threatened.

However, her resolve to reach the top came in mid-1993 when the cops brutally dragged her out of the Writers' Building, which houses the CM's office in Kolkata. She was union minister in the Narasimha Rao government and was demanding justice for a disabled girl, a rape victim. Mamata wanted to meet the CM Jyoti Basu, who was then heading the Communist Party of India (Marxist) government.

It was a cold night and while sitting on a dharna, she had taken a resolve to enter the Writers' Building only after she had ousted CPM from power. Eighteen years later, in 2011, she had walked into the Writers' Building as CM, demolishing the CPM's fort into irreparable pieces. Her uninterrupted but tenuous political journey has continued till date. Jyoti Basu's tenure was of twenty-three years and 137 days.

> Mamata had earned her place as a leader in West Bengal through her relentless battles, often as a victim of violence, against, not only the CPI(M) but also against her peers and seniors in the Congress. (Jayanta Ghosal *Mamata: Beyond 2021*, translated from Bengali by Arunava Sinha)

The 34-year-long CPI(M) regime, acclaimed as the longest serving in the world, finally ended, and the party has never been able to return to power till date.

In the 2024 Lok Sabha elections, the BJP emerged as a bigger challenger to Mamata than the CPI(M). While Mamata had bagged twenty-nine of the forty-two Lok Sabha seats, polling 45.76 per cent of the votes, the BJP won twelve seats by securing 38.73 per cent votes. The Left Front failed to open its account, while the Congress could pick only one seat. Together, they mustered 11.03 per cent votes.

Mamata and her TMC will, most likely, remain a force to reckon with for years to come, as the Congress and the Communists do not show any signs of revival in West Bengal. The BJP, however, gives her a scare from time to time.

Jayalalithaa was despised by her colleagues when she was ruthlessly climbing the AIADMK ladder under MGR's mentorship. She had first displayed her tenacity to win tough situations at the age of thirty-nine.

An unpleasant incident happened at MGR's funeral procession. She was heckled and pushed out of the vehicle carrying his body to the cremation site amidst the chaos. People had yelled and questioned her about her relationship with MGR.

Jayalalithaa displayed a steely resolve. No tears rolled down her cheeks, and neither did she move an inch from her position. She stood her ground behind his mortal remains, eventually winning his legacy after a brief spell of infighting with MGR's wife Janaki, who also staked claim to his legacy. The grim scene was extensively reported by the media.

'Politics is poison,' Sonia Gandhi had once told her son, Rahul Gandhi. It's a hard truth as people follow success while deserting failures and they are often unkind to women politicians. What MGR's wife Janaki couldn't do, Jayalalithaa did by defeating political rivals, namely DMK and bringing MGR's party to power.

It was in 1989 when Jayalalithaa was literally disrobed by an opposition member during an altercation between the ruling DMK and Jayalalithaa-led AIADMK on the floor of the Tamil Nadu State Assembly. The member pulled her saree, while AIADMK members were escorting her out of the unruly house. Jayalalithaa had then taken another resolve to enter the state assembly only after she headed the state as CM. Jayalalithaa did not have to wait for long, as she was back in the assembly in two years' time.

Mayawati had to lock herself in her room in the UP Guest House to protect herself from irate SP MLAs. She had withdrawn support to the Samajwadi Party-Bahujan Samaj Party coalition government in the state after striking a deal with the Congress and the BJP.

The SP-BSP alliance had won the 1993 State Assembly elections and formed a government under the leadership of Chief Minister Mulayam Singh Yadav. Kanshi Ram and Mayawati monitored the functioning of the government.

The BJP was desperate to break the caste coalition of the two parties, as it was detrimental to their political health and they were keen to reap the benefits of their Ram temple movement. The disputed structure was demolished by a frenzied mob of Kar Sevaks on 6 December 1992.

The BJP had dangled carrots and Mayawati fell for them. While her party legislators were waiting for Mayawati's directions, some SP leaders barged into the State Guest House and forcibly took them to the CM's bungalow, which SP leaders denied, saying that the BSP MLAs had gone there on their own.

Mayawati returned to the State Guest House and locked herself in her room. After much drama, Governor Moti Lal Vora decided to dismiss the Mulayam government and instal Mayawati as CM. In a late-night swearing in ceremony, Mayawati became the first Dalit woman CM of UP in 1995. Prime Minister PV Narasimha Rao had described the moment as a 'miracle of Indian democracy,' even as her supporters saw a future PM in her.

A senior officer who used to work closely with Mayawati told me recently that the State Guest House incident had left an indelible sense of insecurity in Mayawati, so much so that when Satish Gujral, famous sculptor and muralist suggested a lush green Ambedkar Memorial with lawns and slopes without any boundary, she had looked aghast.

Immediately turning down the proposal, Mayawati had said, 'Mulayam would send his cows and buffaloes to destroy the lawns without boundaries.' As she kept pressuring him to raise the height of the walls, Satish Gujral had quietly withdrawn from the project.

Mayawati today fears both open spaces as well as jail, which was triggered by CBI notices to her brother Anand Kumar in corruption cases.

She suffers from paranoia and has restricted her access to party workers as well as the public.

Struggle for power

After Mamata had defeated the CPI(M) stalwart Somnath Chatterjee in 1984, the spotlight shifted on the firebrand lady, who passionately organised protests, demonstrations and dharnas on public issues.

People, till date, remember her daring act of dancing on the bonnet of Jayaprakash Narayan's car, who was popularly known as JP and Lok Nayak, in 1977 during his visit to Kolkata, protesting against the emergency. She was a member of the Congress party then.

Mamata worked with three Prime Ministers—PV Narasimha Rao, 1991 (Congress), Atal Bihari Vajpayee 1999 (BJP) and Dr Manmohan Singh 2004 (Congress). She has been member of both the national conglomerates—United Progressive Alliance and National Democratic Alliance.

She quit the Congress on an anti-corruption plank and had formed TMC on 1 January 1998. She became CM in 2011 and continues to rule the state till date, winning both the 2016 and 2021 Assembly polls. She is now gearing up for the 2026 Assembly Polls.

Mamata played a key role in uniting the fragmented opposition parties before the 2024 Lok Sabha polls, as she held the view that a direct contest between the BJP and joint opposition candidates would turn the tables on NDA.

Her formula was clear—the stronger party should get more seats and support from others in their respective states. She had also advocated for a common political agenda, but the contentious issue of leadership created an exodus of the Bihar CM and JD(U) leader Nitish Kumar from the opposition alliance. He re-joined the NDA to become a part of the Modi government at the Centre.

In her home state, the Congress had no option but to play

second fiddle to Mamata as it had lost much of its base to TMC.

Though Mamata was facing the heat from a resurgent Modi on the saleable plank of appeasement of minorities, she played the game intelligently and won the battle. Now she is taking care of the temples in her state to deprive the BJP of its religious plank.

Post-elections, Mamata may do some fine balancing even if it gets her a tag of political infidelity. West Bengal faces paucity of funds and the Narendra Modi government may need her support to augment its numerical strength in the Lok Sabha. Regional parties do extend issue-based support to rickety governments in their hour of crisis. But at home, she would try to further break the already demoralised BJP.

As such, West Bengal remains the mainstay of her politics although she harbours national ambitions. There would be flip flops as she could temporarily mollify the Central Government if it suits her party and plans. But she will also protect her turf.

BJP has been consistently accusing her of pampering Muslims. Her government constructed a new Jagannath temple in Digha which was inaugurated by Mamata, which many saw as a balancing act. Mamata fears BJP will penetrate the Hindu vote bank and she is determined to plug it before the 2026 Assembly polls. The polls are critical for her political future and of TMC.

Ahead of the 2024 polls, the BJP had challenged her claim of '*Ma, Mati and Manush* (Mother, Land and People),' by raising the Sandeshkhali issue, but they failed.

The then union minister Smriti Irani, who had suffered a humiliating defeat against Rahul Gandhi's manager, KL Sharma in Amethi Lok Sabha constituency, had raised the issue of sexual abuse of women by TMC supporters. She had questioned both Mamata Banerjee and Rahul Gandhi for their silence. TMC-Congress were reluctant poll partners in West Bengal.

Sandeshkhali in North 24 Parganas was on the boil since January 2024 with people demanding action against TMC leader Sheikh Shahjahan and his supporters over allegations of land grabbing and sexual assault. He was later arrested by the CBI. Prime Minister Narendra Modi had also flown down to Kolkata to meet the women victims in Barasat. In a scathing attack onTMC and Mamata, he had said, 'In Mamata's rule, women are being tortured.'

TMC feared that Mamata would lose the precious support of women voters. But before the polling date, two videos surfaced in which two women said they were coerced to make false complaints of rape against the TMC leader. A sting operation had also revealed the complaints were filed on the orders of BJP leaders. Mamata easily won the elections.

In ten months since the protests were held in Sandeshkhali, Mamata made her first visit in the end of December 2024 with a message, 'Do not allow unscrupulous people to exploit you, do not use bribe and buy benefit of state-run welfare schemes as it is your right.'

Mamata's politics has always been full of histrionics, like tying a shawl around her neck, threatening to tie a noose or throwing her shawl on the railway minister Ram Vilas Paswan to protest against neglect of her state in 1997.

Her detractors describe her as whimsical and loud, but people, especially women of her state, love her.

MGR floated AIADMK in 1972 after he was thrown out of DMK by Karunanidhi. Jayalalithaa was MGR's co-star in several films and became member of the party in 1982. She soon proved her mettle and became the propaganda secretary. Seniors had disliked her rise in the party.

MGR decided to send Jayalalithaa to the Rajya Sabha from

1984 to 1989 as he needed someone who was articulate and a linguist to mediate between him and New Delhi. From late Prime Minister Indira Gandhi to renowned author Khushwant Singh, many lawmakers were impressed by the clarity in her maiden speech in the Rajya Sabha. Singh who was a fellow Rajya Sabha member had described her as a lady with beauty and brains.

Jayalalithaa had won her maiden assembly election in 1989 and became the leader of the opposition. She was the youngest CM in 1991 and completed her full term. Her tenure was marked by corruption charges and AIADMK lost the 1996 Assembly elections. She was arrested in a disproportionate asset case. Thereafter, AIADMK and DMK rotated power and after her conviction, Jayalalithaa remained in and out of jail.

Jayalalithaa led her party to victory in 2001. She took the oath of office and secrecy, but again resigned after 130 days. She handed the chair to her loyalist, O Paneerselvam, but was back as CM in 2002 and completed the remaining term till 2006. She lost the 2006 elections to DMK, only to make a comeback in 2011. Jayalalithaa was unseated again after she was held guilty in a DA case. OPS, her hardcore loyalist, was back on the chair. In the elections held in 2016, Jayalalithaa made a comeback, though many had written her off.

In her victory speech, widely reported by the media, she had said, 'Even when ten parties allied themselves against me, I did not have a coalition and I placed my faith in God and built an alliance with the people. It is clear that the people have faith in me and I have total faith in the people.'

She became CM on 23 May 2016 and died of cardiac arrest in December, the same year. OPS became CM the next day, but after seventy-two days in office, he was replaced by Edappadi K Palaniswamy (EPS), who completed the remaining tenure till 6

May 2021 and now heads the party.

Jayalalithaa's interest remained in the welfare of Tamil Nadu and she used her offices to garner funds from the Centre. She used to meet the Prime Ministers and the Cabinet ministers with the state's data on her finger tips.

After her death on 5 December 2016, Congress leader Jairam Ramesh wrote in an article:

> 'Pranab Mukherjee, the deputy chairman of the Planning Commission described her as a master of facts. She visited Delhi to discuss annual plans and had facts and figures at her finger tips and a phenomenal memory. She was an administrator with a strong social conscience. While Rao saw Jayalalithaa as a tantrum thrower, Manmohan Singh praised her administrative skills, gender empowerment and mid-day meal scheme.' (Jairam Ramesh, *Hindustan Times*, 7 December 2016)

Perhaps Jayalalithaa even outgrew her mentor MGR in popularity, as she had never compromised with the interests of the state. People called her supreme leader with dictatorial tendencies.

Jayalalithaa had also emerged as a key player on the national scene as she helped NDA in the formation of the government headed by Atal Bihari Vajpayee which had lasted thirteen months. She was instrumental in its collapse, too.

In 1999, the NDA government had to face a no trust motion after AIADMK withdrew support following its refusal to dismiss the DMK government headed by Karunanidhi. The NDA government lost the motion by one vote.

Jayalalithaa remained CM for fourteen years and 124 days, more than her mentor MGR's tenure of ten years and sixty-five days.

She was sixty-eight years old when death took her away in 2016, leaving several unanswered questions about her personal as well as professional life. She was an enigma, who apparently was not ruffled by controversies and corruption charges that haunted her till she lived.

Jayalalithaa was hailed for her governance and schemes like Amma Canteen. She was incredibly respected by party workers who gave her the names 'Amma' (mother) and '*Puratchi Thalaivi*' (revolutionary leader).

The 'Queen of Tamil Cinema' lived two lives—one for the public, and a friendless, lonely life in her private quarters. In office, she did not tolerate criticism or suggestions from colleagues or senior partymen. She loved loyalty and sycophancy.

Party men and women falling at her feet or waiting for her helicopter to land with hands folded in reverence was their strategy to gain proximity to power. AIADMK, a one-time strong regional party, has now started losing ground.

> As it is a party in which all power is concentrated in a supreme leader, with no second-rung leadership—an AIADMK leader famously said—MGR was "number one," and the rest of the party consisted of "zeroes," implying that without the leader, the rest meant nothing. This trend continued during Jayalalithaa's tenure as well. Its fortunes are linked to the individual heading it, and the organisation of millions of members and grassroots functionaries appear lost in the absence of a powerful and charismatic leader.
>
> (K Venkataramanan, *The Hindu*, 5 February 2023)

EPS, who heads the AIADMK is not from the world of cinema. He is a hardcore politician, determined to keep AIADMK alive. The party is unlikely to die soon.

Once upon a time, Mayawati was such a terror that mafiosi as well as party detractors were afraid to discuss her even in private conversations. She would spare none while engineering their electoral defeats.

Mayawati last tasted power in 2007, but has continued to live an inaccessible life, in an ivory tower. As Enforcement Directorate and Central Bureau of Investigation had raided homes of the high and mighty and incarcerated even CMs, Mayawati decided to play safe after her brother was summoned in a corruption case.

It is hard to believe that she is the same firebrand Mayawati, who publicly lambasted both her opponents, Congress and SP as well as her poll partners, including senior BJP leaders, Atal Bihari Vajpaee, Kalyan Singh and LK Advani, while whimsically snapping alliances.

Mayawati often said that she has neither got power in legacy nor it was bestowed by any destiny. 'The success has come from sheer hard work and determination. I fully believe that success comes neither free nor it is automatic.' The BSP now is in the doldrums with no young leadership to struggle on the streets while the fainthearted Mayawati strategises at home. But it has a captive vote bank, which believed in BSP's mission and wanted to see Mayawati as PM of the country one day. Was it actually a movement, or did it start as a mission, which drifted midway as they chased power?

Chapter 6

Rising Regional Sons and Daughters Eye the Throne

On 22 August 2024, Congress President Mallikarjun Kharge and Rahul Gandhi met the National Conference leaders, Farooq Abdullah and his son Omar Abdullah at the latter's residence in Srinagar to discuss an electoral alliance for the historic elections in 2024, the first after the abrogation of Article 370 in August 2019, which withdrew the special status granted to J&K.

The political parties were keen to test the waters in an emerging political scenario, where citizens saw an opportunity to deliver a referendum on the Central Government's decision. They wanted restoration of statehood after its demotion to a Union Territory.

The scions, under the guidance of their seniors, comfortably sealed poll issues and the seat sharing pact in an atmosphere of camaraderie as the relationship between the two families, the Gandhis and the Abdullahs, dates back to three generations, albeit dotted with sporadic political skirmishes.

Both the Congress and the National Conference were founded before India had attained Independence, the Congress in 1885 and the National Conference in 1932—and their leaders, Jawaharlal Nehru and Sheikh Abdullah, went on to become the first Prime Ministers of India and Kashmir respectively. The head of J&K was originally called Prime Minister, and it was only after 1965 that the position was renamed as Chief Minister.

In both families, the political legacy was inherited by the children. In Congress, the position of President was held largely by members of the Nehru-Gandhi family with some non-Gandhi Presidents in 1929, and briefly in 1946 and after Independence in 1951. Nehru became Congress President in 1946 and the baton was passed on to Indira Gandhi, who then passed it to son Rajiv Gandhi. After his death, it went to Sonia Gandhi and later to her son, Rahul. Mallikarjun Kharge was elected President in 2022, but Rahul remains the face of the party.

Sheikh Abdullah was succeeded by his son Farooq Abdullah, who remains the President of the National Conference, while the inheritor of his political legacy, his son Omar Abdullah is Vice President and CM of the Union Territory.

Kashmir's main Opposition party, the J&K People's Democratic Party, was founded by Mufti Mohammed Sayeed in 1999 and after his death in 2016, his daughter Mehbooba Mufti became its undisputed President. Now her daughter Iltija Mufti who is thirty-four has entered politics and is striving to build her independent vision for the region to chart her own course.

She started her career as political adviser to her mother, but lost her maiden election from the family seat of Srigufwara-Bijbehara in the 2024 Lok Sabha elections. She may succeed Mehbooba.

Significantly, the first crucial election in the most sensitive border state of Jammu and Kashmir was led by the regional parties and their dynasts.

Prime Minister Narendra Modi led the campaign holding dynastic politics responsible for increased terrorism and lack of development in the border state. He had said that 'The political parties you trusted did not care about your children, as they were promoting their own children. They did not allow new leadership to develop.'

Omar Abdullah responded after winning the state assembly elections. He said, 'Dynastic politics is not a lifelong ticket to success. I lost the Lok Sabha election, but won the State polls. I am the same person, from the same family and same political party.'

NC has largely dominated the state's politics, ruling it for forty years while PDP ran the government for one term of five years. Among the national parties, the Congress ruled the state for about fourteen years and, thereafter, turned into an ally of either of the two regional parties. The PDP-Congress had formed a government by rotation in 2002, but PDP withdrew support before completion of its full term. The state saw five coalition governments since 1947, and only one could complete its term.

To get a toehold in state politics, the BJP also formed a coalition government with the PDP from 2015 to 2018. After that the disturbed state remained under President's rule till 2024, when a new Kashmir participated in both the Lok Sabha and the State Assembly polls under the Indian national flag. While the BJP performed well in Hindu-dominated Jammu region, the NC-Congress alliance formed the government after their spectacular performance in Kashmir. The PDP was decimated.

After some gains in Jammu, the BJP is now aspiring to crack the Valley and put an end to dynastic rule in the border state. Can they?

NC and PDP are deeply entrenched in the Valley, whereas the BJP is still struggling to find a toehold.

> As a third-generation politician and a leader of the National Conference, Omar Abdullah's journey is one of both inherited responsibility and personal tenacity. ...Despite challenges, his leadership was marked by efforts to improve infrastructure,

> promote tourism, and foster education initiatives. With his father, Farooq Abdullah, stepping back from active leadership, the mantle of leading the National Conference has firmly fallen on Omar's shoulders.'
>
> (India News Desk, *Financial Express*, 9 October 2024)

Omar entered politics at the young age of 28 years, winning the Lok Sabha election in 1998 and became Union Minister of State in the NDA government headed by Atal Bihari Vajpayee. He made his debut in the state assembly in 2002 and became CM at the age of 38 years in 2008.

He has once again taken charge of the state at a time when the aspirations of people in the strife-torn state are high and their first expectation from him is to bargain with an unobliging Centre for the restoration of statehood. His future as CM, and that of his party, now hinges on this contentious issue as the BJP-led NDA government is unlikely to oblige him.

Public expectations from Omar were summed up by *Kashmir Horizon's* Mohammad Irfan in this report from 13 October 2024:

> Omar's upbringing in a politically charged environment laid the groundwork for his own future in politics. His vision for the state is rooted in the belief that democratic governance is essential for progress and stability. He has long advocated for dialogue among all stakeholders, emphasising the need for a nuanced understanding of the region's complexities. His commitment to transparency and accountability in governance will play a critical role in rebuilding trust between the government and the people.'
>
> As the first Chief Minister of the newly formed Union Territory, Abdullah has the opportunity to redefine the relationship

between the people of Jammu and Kashmir and the Central Government. His leadership style, characterised by a blend of traditional values and modern governance practices, could serve as a blueprint for future leaders in the region.

Omar's every move is under the scanner as people have given him a clear mandate in the state assembly, allowing him to start confidently, without fear of any clandestine moves to destabilise his government.

Soon after the formation of the government, his local rival Mehbooba Mufti wrote in the monthly newsletter *Speak UP*: 'Governing J&K would require delicate dance with New Delhi. In J&K, winning an election might be the simplest part of the political journey.'

The first woman CM of J&K and the last CM of the erstwhile state, highlighted the public issues to be addressed. She advised the BJP to adopt a more conciliatory approach. She, as their erstwhile partner in governance, knows them best.

After the death of her father, Mehbooba had headed the coalition government with the BJP from 2016-2018, the price of which she paid in 2024. People did not approve of the PDP-BJP coalition, which was termed as a meeting of North Pole and South Pole and had fallen under the weight of their ideological contradictions.

PDP lost all the three Lok Sabha seats, while the party, in its worst performance in the state since its formation 25 years back, suffered a rout winning barely three assembly seats.

The J&K results also manifest the distinct choices people make in the state assembly and Lok Sabha elections. Both the strong regional leaders and former J&K CMs, Omar Abdullah and Mehbooba Mufti, had lost the national elections, but in the state polls, people, in search of a stable government, voted NC to power in a clear-cut verdict. Omar had lost the Baramullah Lok Sabha seat to an independent candidate Sheikh Abdullah Rashid, who has been behind bars since 2019 under the Unlawful Activities (Prevention) Act (UAPA) on charges of funding terrorists.

Mehbooba lost the Anantnagar-Rajouri seat to NC. Of the five Lok Sabha seats in the state, the BJP and NC won two each, while one went to an Independent.

A law graduate, who worked in a bank and then in an airline, before entering politics in 1996, Mehbooba is credited with having nurtured the PDP which her father Mufti Mohammad had founded in 1999. Her father was always clear that he would transfer the mantle to his daughter, who went through her own struggles in a volatile state, braving threats and detentions.

Before his demise in January 2016, Mufti Mohd Sayeed had described his daughter as efficient, as one who built the party, is well-connected with the masses and is talented enough to run the state. In 2002, barely three years after its formation, PDP had formed government in alliance with the Congress. It also emerged as the single largest party in the J&K Assembly in 2014.

Mufti's son, Tassaduq Mufti, a cinematographer, acclaimed for his work in popular Bollywood films *Omkara* and *Kaminey*, joined PDP in 2017, on the day of his father's first death anniversary. He said that he stands firmly with his sister Mehbooba and the family would be working together. Mehbooba had warmly welcomed him into the party, presenting Mufti's dearest son to the public. Junior Mufti, till then, had not shown any interest in politics.

Now in 2024, PDP, which many believe was a strong alternative to NC, is facing an existential crisis. Several founder members have deserted the party after the abrogation of Article

370. People felt that the PDP-BJP alliance in 2014 helped the latter get a foothold in the state.

Mehbooba is now left with no option but to wait for the elections five years later. Till then she can only try and dispel the perception about her proximity to the BJP. The challenge before her is as huge as her loss in the polls.

Her daughter Iltija is trying to do some damage control by her vitriol against BJP's agenda. She recently described Hindutva as a disease, evoking sharp reactions from the Hindu brigade, but her remark must have assuaged the hurt sentiments of the Muslim community facing saffron heat in the country. In a bid to distance herself from PDP's mistakes, she always insists that she is Mehbooba's daughter but has an identity of her own.

North or South, the young have taken control of prominent regional parties from Kashmir to Kanyakumari and are driving right or left in search of political sustenance. The sons and a few daughters are rising despite the labels and titles. They are taking decisions as situations demand, not necessarily from the rule book written by their parents. They have inherited the legacy along with the follies.

It's BJP vs. young Turks in the north

The two young Yadav chieftains of North India, 51-year-old Akhilesh Yadav and 35-year-old Tejashwi Yadav have inherited a rich legacy from their respective fathers, late Mulayam Singh Yadav, who founded Samajwadi Party in Uttar Pradesh in 1992 and Lalu Prasad Yadav, who formed the Rashtriya Janata Dal in Bihar in 1997.

The senior Yadavs, belonging to a backward caste had embarked on their political journey when the politics of the country was largely dominated by Brahmins. They were politically ambivalent, impulsive and sometimes volatile while clearing caste barriers.

With their rustic apolitical background, they connected with the rural masses, but lacked the sophistication to charm the urban crowd. They earned several uncomplimentary titles, but they remained a force till Mulayam aged and Lalu was jailed in corruption cases.

UP and Bihar together contribute 120 of the 543 Lok Sabha seats in Indian Parliament, and this is the underlying factor behind their importance in the country's politics. The two states were the epicentre of the Mandal movement and both Mulayam and Lalu are its two off shoots.

Before his death, Mulayam completed the succession process, anointing his son Akhilesh as his legal heir. He is the National President of the Samajwadi Party. Mulayam's Bihar counterpart, Lalu Yadav started the succession process but stopped short of holding the crowning ceremony. Tejashwi Yadav is the undeclared successor of Lalu Yadav and is currently the vice president of the RJD. Ideologically, both parties practice and preach social justice and secularism.

Akhilesh and Tejashwi have inherited a solid base of loyal voters and a committed cadre, a well-oiled organisational machinery with infrastructure spread from booth to the state level. But they have also inherited a baggage of bitterness and their party's sullied image.

Despite their own personal goodwill, both the young scions have been left to fight a tough battle to change the perceptions of their parties, that they pander to Muslims and the mafia.

Akhilesh is judicious while commenting on his father's style of functioning. He says, 'They took decisions that the circumstances of the day demanded. After all, much water has flowed down the Ganga since then.'

Tejashwi, on the other hand, had offered an apology for RJD's past mistakes, projecting himself as a symbol of *Nayi Soch, Naya Bharat*—New Vision, New India.

Once when Akhilesh was asked to comment on how he would change public perception about the Samajwadi Party badgered by the BJP as a party of goondas, he had said: 'By honest hard work without diluting the party's ideology. The challenge before the party is to strike a balance between social engineering, social justice and social prosperity in line with socialist Ram Manohar Lohia's slogan, "Socialism is prosperity with equality and empowerment".'

Both the young leaders, who have pledged social justice, have taken forward the battle of secularism vs communalism, which had peaked in the 1990s during the Ram temple and Mandal movements.

Since then, the politics of the country has undergone a sea-change with Prime Minister Narendra Modi sweeping the General Elections in 2014, 2019 and 2024, by offering a heady mix of Hindutva and development.

In this context, Akhilesh's battle is tougher than Tejashwi's as he faces the saffron-robed CM of UP Yogi Adityanath, pursuing his polarising agenda and winning the largest state in 2017 and 2022. Bihar still has Nitish Kumar as CM, whose party Janata Dal(U), also espouses a socialist and secular ideology.

Since Akhilesh slowed down the double-engine government led by Modi-Yogi in the 2024 General Elections by winning thirty-seven of the eighty Lok Sabha seats, he is now their *bete noire* number one.

UP's loss had a severe impact on the BJP's winning tally. It caused huge humiliation to the party, which lost the Ayodhya-

Faizabad Lok Sabha seat even after the grand inauguration of the Ram Temple in Ayodhya on 22 January 2024, months before the country went to the polls. The BJP leadership was confident of riding the temple wave in a majority of the eighty constituencies in the state. The loss of seats in UP pulled down BJP's national tally, compelling it to borrow support from TDP and JD(U) from Andhra Pradesh and Bihar to form the government for the third consecutive term.

Akhilesh emerged as the new hero of the Opposition bloc with his elevation from a state party to the third largest party in the Indian Parliament. He became an eyesore for the BJP, larger than even his father Mulayam. The war of words between Yogi Adityanath and Akhilesh is reminiscent of the Kalyan-Mulayam spats. Kalyan Singh was BJP CM during the Ram temple movement when Mulayam was heading the Opposition.

Today, Akhilesh is counted as the tallest backward leader of the state who, like his father, would play a crucial role in national politics in the years to come. The BJP union minister Jyotiraditya Scindia was candid enough to admit this.

Akhilesh had carefully crafted the election plan for 2024 as it was the first after the death of his father Mulayam Singh Yadav in October 2022. Earlier, when he had managed to improve the party's tally in the 425-member State Assembly, his father had been around.

In one stroke, the Yadav scion silenced his detractors, both within the party and outside, even as they discussed publicly how Akhilesh was not a patch on Mulayam. But after the 2024 polls, they started singing paeans about how he had come of age.

Akhilesh refuses to get dragged into any debate that compares him with his father as he himself eulogises Mulayam, not only as his father but also as Netaji. He had learnt politics watching his father's every move—from his commendations and condemnations in private and in public.

His biggest challenge was to change the party's image and broaden its support base, till now limited to Muslims and Yadavs, by crafting a new strategy. He knew he had to take on the mighty BJP and its Hindutva agenda and fight a pitched ideological war at a time when saffron has captured the imagination of the people. And, at the same time, he has to protect and support his constituency.

He first devised the PDA formula, bringing *Pichra* (Backward), Dalit (Scheduled Caste) and *Alpasankhyak* (Minorities) to the fore of his politics. He took this beyond speeches and translated it into action by building social alliances. His second poll weapon was the caste census, which he said his government would conduct, as and when they were voted to power. But the Centre has announced the caste census to hijack the opposition's potent issue and weaken the PDA tool.

Simultaneously, he played a crucial role in the construction of the Opposition bloc I.N.D.I.A, despite SP's long-term differences with the Congress. UP was the first state to seal a seat-sharing pact with poll partners. His efforts paid huge dividends. After humbling the BJP, he said, 'I did not win the seats because I am a dynast but because we had a strategy.'

Akhilesh always cites the famous quote on post-poll bouquets and brickbats, 'Success has many fathers, defeat has none.'

Akhilesh has cleared the preliminaries, but the finals, which are two years away in 2027, would be more challenging for him. BJP has taken an aggressive Sanatani route to reconsolidate the Hindu vote bank that had collapsed in 2024 and are also aiming to divide the minorities by hook or by crook. His challenge would be to maintain the 2024 momentum, which has apparently faded as the BJP won its first challenge in the by-elections.

Akhilesh has started his homework and his wife Dimple Yadav has emerged as his eyes and ears. His daughter, Aditi is all set to take a plunge in politics. The large family of the family man, as he is called, has also reunited.

Mulayam sent his son to the best of schools—from Military School, Dholpur, to Sydney for a Masters in Environmental Engineering. However, he was unsure about the political acumen of his unassuming son, as he had to bat on the political turf of the largest state with the highest political stakes. He often wondered if his son would be able to take forward the Samajwadi Party and its ideological battle against the BJP.

Akhilesh, who like his father, has never allied with the BJP, admits the challenges before him, as mainstream parties would not want regional parties to grow at their cost, in the country's largest state, as they weaken the national parties. However, till now, they have failed to stop them in UP, where the main fight of the mainstream parties is with regional parties.

The fight has now narrowed down between the BJP and the SP after a sharp decline in the electoral fortunes of the other regional force, the Bahujan Samaj Party. Another national party, the Congress, is also not in the race as of now and in all probability, it may contest the elections with the SP.

Akhilesh defines his two challenging priorities—the 2027 Assembly Polls and evolving the winning formula which would include good candidates, PDA, caste census and a strong ideological stand. The second priority is to fulfil Netaji's dream of SP growing into a national party.

SP cadres are getting restless as they want their very own Tipu to be Sultan once again!

Tejashwi Yadav

Rashtriya Janata Dal National President Lalu Yadav was neither amused nor angered by Bihar Chief Minister Nitish Kumar's jibe during the 2024 polls, questioning his large family rather than scams at an election rally.

Since 1997, when Lalu went to jail in the multi-crore Fodder Scam, handing over the CM's chair to his wife Rabri Devi, poll rallies have never been complete without corruption sneers aimed at him. However, this time the Bihar CM chose to ridicule him for producing nine children saying, 'Should one have so many children?'

Former CM Rabri Devi retorted, 'He (Nitish) can't handle one son. He has a problem with us having nine children. He should know we run our family as well as the state.'

Lalu with nine children had chosen his youngest son Tejashwi as his heir apparent, but delayed the formal coronation to protect both the party and the family from internecine troubles.

People and the party have accepted Tejashwi as Lalu's heir as he has been given a free hand to run the show. A cautious Lalu is buying time, though none of his nine children would disobey him till he is around. Misa is ambitious and Lalu has prudently sent her to the Lok Sabha.

The actual game in large political families often starts after the satrap has passed away, as opponents fan ambitions in relatives, like in the case of Aparna Yadav (SP) and Ajit Pawar (NCP), both of whom have joined the BJP.

Tej Pratap is unpredictable, but can team up with Misa. Political observers in Bihar foresee a battle in the family if Lalu fails to complete the succession process in his lifetime.

Both of Lalu's sons have inherited his eloquence and are fiery orators, but Tej Pratap's idiosyncrasies like blowing a conch shell before addressing a meeting or visiting temples, make him unsuitable for the chair.

The Bihar Assembly polls, to be held in October or November 2025, will be a do-or-die battle for Tejashwi Yadav as he, along with his weak poll partner, the Congress, will be facing a robust BJP-JD(U)-Lok Janshakti combine, which won thirty of the forty Lok Sabha seats in 2024 and rules both the Centre and the State.

In the opposition bloc, the RJD won four out of the twenty-three seats it contested, an improvement from zero in 2019, Congress three out of nine, and CPI (ML) two and Independent one. In the 2020 Assembly elections, NDA won 125 seats and formed the government, while the Mahagatbandhan trailed with 110 seats. He missed the CM's chair by twelve seats in a keenly contested poll.

Can Tejashwi Yadav drive RJD to power and win back its dominance in the state in 2025? This will decide his future as well as that of the party he is leading.

In the 2024 Lok Sabha elections, Tejashwi had adopted two strategies. First, he built unemployment as his main plank which attracted the youth towards the RJD.

Second, he tried to expand his support base of Yadavs and Muslims by floating the A-Z formula, opening the doors of the party for all castes and communities. The image makeover bid failed, as the decision did not reflect in ticket distribution. Apparently, Lalu took most of the decisions, while many considered Tejashwi responsible for the party's defeat.

Tejashwi again has an opportunity in 2025, but he will have to counter his opponents, like Prime Minister Narendra Modi, who described him as the 'yuvraj of a jungle party,' reminding people of lawlessness during Lalu's rule.

There are other challenges, too. Writing in the *Indian Express*,

Pushpendra highlights three challenges:

> First he will get rid of the double stigma of being a 'dynast' and inheriting a political legacy widely seen as "jungle raj" when his parents helmed the state for a good 15 years. Second, Tejashwi needs to carry forward a new vision and agenda for Bihar's development, building upon but not confined to largely worn-out "social justice." During his brief stint as the state's deputy chief minister, he tried to demonstrate his potential by delivering on two fronts—government jobs and caste census. Third, Tejashwi will have to show maturity in nurturing the opposition coalition. The unease in the coalition is apparent as he does not want his "friendly" rivals to grow substantially. The lack of regular communication and meetings with coalition partners is conspicuous and does not help create trust between their specific social bases. (*Indian Express*, 28 January 2025)

Lalu declared Tejashwi the CM face of RJD at the party's national executive meeting in January 2025. He has been touring the state, drawing large crowds, raising correct public issues, but is beset with a weak partner in the Congress.

He is smart in taking on the BJP's Hindutva propaganda at public rallies, asking how Hindus could be in danger when the country is being ruled by a Hindu PM and a Hindu Home Minister, Narendra Modi and Amit Shah, and when the chiefs of three wings of the Defence Forces are Hindus.

And then he raises the burning issue of unemployment and caste census. 'They say we are distributing rations, anyone can do this work. Why can't they provide jobs?' he asks.

Lalu realises he brings in thousands of votes in every constituency as he has cultivated loyal voters and cadre. But he also knows he remains the party's biggest liability and is thus taking a back seat. However, Tejashwi will have to make some changes in the party organisation to shed its image of a Yadav party that has been promoting criminals and corruption, by inducting fresh faces, but this would require fine balancing.

Tejashwi would require a foolproof strategy to crack the 2025 polls, as Nitish Kumar with his image and BJP with its infrastructure, are formidable combinations. However, what goes in favour of Tejashwi is the growing quest for change evident in the state, tired of Nitish Kumar's twenty-year rule.

He is young and connects easily with the rural masses, irrespective of their age. A campaign around young leadership can help him turn the tables on the BJP, which had used Naveen Patnaik's age and ill health to oust him from the comfortable chair of CM.

Tejashwi is a class nine dropout, who wanted to make cricket his profession, and with a dream to represent the Indian national cricket team, someday. He was Delhi Captain for Under-15s and Under-17s national teams. He played in the Under-19 team when Virat Kohli was its captain.

One morning, after a visit to the RJD office with his father, Tejashwi decided to play politics and rest his cricket bat, little realising that the political turf is thorny. Senior Bihar politician Shambhu Srivastava has closely seen the politics of Bihar. He says that while the regional parties have formed majority governments in Uttar Pradesh—BSP in 2007 and SP in 2012, the JD(U) and RJD have never won a majority in the state assembly and would always need support to form a government in Bihar. As of now, the two national parties would play second fiddle to them.

The political dynamics would nonetheless change after the 2025 polls. The LJP would stay, while JD(U) may start to wither away after Nitish is not around. RJD may also suffer splits engineered by the BJP—but only after Lalu is not there and

Tejashwi loses the 2025 battle.

But none of the regional parties will completely die.

Akash Anand

'A young supporter of Baba Saheb's vision, I stand for Education, Empowerment, and Equality.' This is how the National Coordinator of the Bahujan Samaj Party, 29-year-old Akash Anand describes himself on his social media accounts. An MBA from London, Akash Anand entered politics in 2017 at the young age of 22. He was groomed for seven years before *Bua* Mayawati declared him her political successor in December 2023, a few months before the Lok Sabha elections.

He is a firebrand, and, in few months, he came under the political spotlight. BSP's core constituency, which was growing amenable to Mayawati's mellowed tone, found her replacement in him as he touched their heart by raising issues of their concern.

Akash had started drawing crowds when Mayawati abruptly removed him from campaigning in UP, while it was heading for the third phase of polling in May 2024. He was also removed from the National Coordinator's position after he was booked by the Sitapur police for violating the model code of conduct. The provocation was his vitriol against the Yogi Adityanath government.

In a fiery speech at an election rally, the video of which went viral, Akash was heard calling the BJP government in UP a bulldozer government and a government of traitors. His statement, 'The party that leaves its youth hungry and enslaves its elderly is a terrorist government. Taliban runs such a government in Afghanistan. The Bharatiya Janata Party at the Centre is a party of thieves; which took Rs 16,000 crore through electoral bonds,' was widely reported in the media.

Loud applause followed. But an FIR was registered by the

Sitapur administration, followed by a sacking order by the party's National President Mayawati. All his rallies were cancelled as Mayawati described him as politically immature. His humiliation did not end there. In March 2025, an intemperate Mayawati expelled Akash from the BSP along with his father-in-law Ashok Siddhartha after he flayed BSP's style of functioning. After few weeks, he was reinstated in the party but his positions were not restored. Since then, he has been lying low.

Interestingly, BSP founder and Mayawati's mentor Kanshi Ram never pulled her back for her controversial utterances against one and all—from the Prime Minister to the Chief Minister and their team members. Such was Kanshi Ram's confidence in her that several senior leaders who were with the BSP since its inception in the 1980s were sacked for opposing her.

Kanshi Ram declared her the National President of the BSP on 15 December 2001 at the Laxman Jhoola Park in Lucknow. Kanshi Ram had seen the fate of the Republican Party of India, which had split into several factions after the death of its creator, BR Ambedkar. This split had adversely impacted the Bahujan movement and Kanshi Ram did not want his party to dissipate and disappear along with the movement.

Akash has accepted Mayawati's diktat without a whisper of protest, though his supporters are disappointed. Akash has softened the tone and tenor of his social media posts and even after his reinduction in the party, he has restricted himself to retweeting Mayawati's messages. The Bahujan Samaj voice has gone missing.

According to party insiders, several names were considered for her successor as she had laid two conditions—the person should be 15 years younger and not from the family. The seniors and trusted lieutenants were not unanimous on any one name.

A loyalist of the party, whose name was also under

consideration, said the senior leaders advised Mayawati to bring someone from the family as people and the party cadre would not accept anyone else. They suggested Akash's name as he was educated and had political acumen.

Insiders said Mayawati gave Akash some political assignments which he accomplished independently. This is how Kanshi Ram had tested Mayawati's political capabilities and once he was convinced that she would be the best person to lead BSP, he decided on her name and brooked no opposition from any quarter. He supported her completely.

Can Mayawati have the same confidence in Akash? She was rattled by the very first complaint against him or did she succumb to BJP's pressures? Akash will have to step into the shoes of a young Mayawati to revive the party.

Akash is the son of Mayawati's brother Anand Kumar, who has stood behind her like a rock, even while facing corruption charges. Investigations are on and hang like a Damocles's sword around his neck.

Mayawati had inherited a growing party, while Akash or any other successor is going to acquire a politically bankrupt party with no representation in the Uttar Pradesh State Assembly or in the Lok Sabha.

The support base is cracking as a phobia-stricken Mayawati is increasingly going invisible. The cadre and the voters are both desperate and disgusted, but they are not deserting the party for Dalits by Dalits. They still see some hope in Akash, who is intelligent and represents the voice of young Dalits.

Paradoxically, where BSP once gave voice to Dalits, today Akash needs that voice to rebuild the party, a one of its kind in the country.

Jayant Chaudhary

The Texas-born graduate from the London School of Economics, 45-year-old Jayant Chaudhary is a look alike of his grandfather, Chaudhary Charan Singh, and that is reason enough for Jats of Western Uttar Pradesh to adore him.

'*Arey woh to Chaudhary jaisa lagta hai, baap pe nahin gaya hai*—he resembles his grandfather and has not gone on his late father Ajit Singh,' they exult.

And when Jayant tenaciously stood with the farmers in 2022, their common refrain was, 'He displays the same temper, speaks the same lingo in the same style as Charan Singh, and is both fiery and witty. Who can say he studied abroad and quit a corporate job before taking charge of RLD?'

An MA in Accounts and Finance, Jayant had, in 2011, said at the *Hindustan Times* Conclave in Lucknow, 'I have grown up reading books authored by my grandfather. His speeches were a study in statistics that brought out the urban bias at the expense of planning and allocation of funds for the countryside. He is my political idol.'

Jats had fully supported his father, Chaudhary Ajit Singh, but were weary of his political dalliances. He got the coveted chairs but lost credibility. Jayant too flipped sides and gave in to the BJP after the NDA government announced a Bharat Ratna for Chaudhary Charan Singh in early 2024. It won them support of both Jayant Chaudhary and the Jats.

Jayant also gained by this move. He became a minister at the Centre, while his party got a berth in the UP Cabinet.

After the arrival of the third generation Chaudhary, Jats had harboured a dream of seeing him in the CM's chair. As of now, they are happy that Jayant is a union minister in the BJP-led government though they are unhappy with Modi. In Jayant, they've found a leader who looks like his grandfather, at times talks the way he did, and has the potential of becoming his party's modern face.

Jayant became RLD president in May 2021. It was a smooth transition from father to son as there were no other claimants. The challenge before him was to expand or recover the shrunk footprints of the party. They had tested pre-poll and post-poll alliances with all parties—the BJP, Congress and SP, and his father was minister in both the NDA and the UPA governments.

RLD was never a pan-UP party, but had pockets of influence in Eastern and Western UP during Charan Singh's days.

The party's best-ever performance in UP Assembly Elections was in 2002 when it won fourteen of the thirty-eight seats the party contested in alliance with the BJP. In 2007, it won ten seats without any ally. In 2012, the party allied with the Congress and won nine seats, but in 2017, it decided to go solo and could win just one seat, Chaprauli in Baghpat. However, the lone MLA dumped RLD in favour of the BJP, post-elections.

In Lok Sabha elections, the RLD won its best ever five seats in the 2009 elections it had contested in alliance with the BJP. It was a gain of two seats over their 2004 performance when it had partnered with SP.

It drew a blank in 2014 as a member of UPA. Both Ajit and Jayant lost their seats—Baghpat and Mathura. In 2019, he joined the grand alliance of SP-Congress-BSP, but the RLD lost all the three seats it contested. Ajit Singh and Jayant Chaudhary were two of the three losers.

Jayant once said, 'People should stop asking me about being a Jat politician. I have been hurt politically in one election. I got so tired of being asked what Jats are going to do, I said I don't know what they will do. Chaudhary Sahab had fervently advocated breaking the hold that caste has on our society. So, I said inter-caste marriages should happen. I got backlash from all *khap* leaders but I will still stick by it because that's what Chaudhary Sahab always stood for. So, I am honouring his legacy. Whether my seats reduce to zero or go up, that's not his legacy.'

Today, the minority community is asking him the same question. Will he stand by them in this hour of crisis?

Chirag Paswan

'Chirag Paswan is like my son, he is the future of Bihar,' said Prime Minister Narendra Modi while campaigning in Bihar in May 2024.

Chirag Paswan who is forty-five had also responded in his tweet, 'PM Modi used to call twice daily when my father Ram Vilas Paswan was hospitalised. During that time, PM Modi took care of me and my family like an elder member of the family. Imagine the Prime Minister of India calling you twice daily, not only with full updates on my father's health but also after seeking second opinion from doctors across the country.'

He had even recalled the bond between PM Modi and his late father. 'Their relationship was very special. Prime Minister Narendra Modi always gave my father love, respect and honour. He now extends the same affection to me. I am inseparable from Prime Minister Modi,' he said.

BJP chose him over his uncle Pashupati Kumar Paras while working on an alliance with the Lok Janshakti Party (LJP), thus validating his claim over the party, which had split into two after the death of its founder Ram Vilas Paswan in October 2020.

His uncle Pashupati Kumar Paras, in a midnight coup in June 2021, had walked out of the party and split it vertically, ousting Chirag from all positions. Chirag soon recovered from the massive jolt and emerged as the only NDA constituent in Bihar with a 100 per cent strike rate in the 2024 Lok Sabha polls. The BJP had given five seats to LJP and he won all. Chirag Paswan has come a long way and is a minister in the Narendra Modi government.

Now he is working on a mission to establish an NDA government in Bihar in the 2025 Assembly elections. In 2019, Ram Vilas Paswan was alive when the party had swept all the six seats BJP had allotted.

His slogan is 'Bihar first and Bihari first.' The actor turned politician has a long way to go. Ram Vilas Paswan, the most popular Dalit leader, formed his own party LJP in 2000 and supposedly broke Dalit voters away from RJD.

Chirag is now the undisputed Dalit leader of Bihar.

Conrad Sangma

In May 2020, a video clip of Meghalaya Chief Minister Conrad K Sangma, who at forty-six was playing the electric guitar went viral. After a hectic three-day in the Assembly session, he wrote on Instagram: 'Unwinding with some Iron Maiden stuff—It's been a long while I haven't played—I made some mistakes.'

Sangma, son of late versatile Lok Sabha Speaker and Chief Minister of Meghalaya, PA Sangma, lost his first elections in 2004 and realised at an early age that while family name could give entry or easy access, it may not always deliver boundaries. He won the 2008 elections and thereafter, despite a turbulent political life, there has been no going back. He is the twelfth Chief Minister of Meghalaya since 2018.

His National People's Party in alliance with NDA lost both the seats, one to Congress and the other to Voice of the People's Party, which was established in 2021.

Interestingly, Prime Minister Narendra Modi and Union Home Minister Amit Shah had attended the swearing in ceremony of the dynast Sangma in March 2023, as their one-time mission was to stop the Congress from forming the government.

A graduate from the Wharton School of Business in the US and Imperial College, University of London, Sangma was elected National President of National People's Party in 2016, after the demise of his father who had founded the party in July 2012 after his expulsion from Nationalist Congress Party. NPP is small, but is a national party.

His two siblings are also in politics, but the succession process went on without any opposition or drama. The party chose him for his dynamic leadership—he connects with people, young and old alike.

The North East with twenty-five Lok Sabha seats has been the bastion of the Congress, which BJP has tried to usurp. However, regional parties remain the choice of the voters keen to protect their identity and culture. They stitch regional alliances as well as with national parties.

> Once the dominant national party, Congress has not been in power in any of the eight States in the Northeast since 2018 when it lost power to the National People's Party (NPP)-led alliance in Meghalaya and the Mizo National Front (MNF) in Mizoram. Led by the BJP with fourteen seats—nine in Assam, two each in Arunachal Pradesh and Tripura, and one in Manipur; the National Democratic Alliance won nineteen seats in 2019.
>
> Congress won four and non-aligned candidates two. (Rahul Karmakar, *The Hindu*, 5 June 2024)

The tally for NDA dipped by three seats in 2024.

For instance, in Mizoram, Zoram Nationalist Party won the lone seat. It had promised independence from national alliances, that had resonated in the elections. In all, there are four regional parties in such a tiny state.

The Manipur results came on expected lines, where the Congress and its ally, National People's Front defeated the BJP. The state has been on the boil since 2023 and the Centre has failed to resolve its ethnic conflict and violence. However, Assam continues to remain the BJP's stronghold.

Hemant Soren

Political psephologist and Founder Director of C-Voters, Yashwant Deshmukh observes, 'One youngster who has surprised me is Hemant Soren; he is one of the most successful politicians. From the legacy perspective also, he took over Jharkhand Mukti Morcha and doubled where his father left.'

Hemant Soren (49) is son of Shibu Soren who co-founded the Jharkhand Mukti Morcha (JMM) in 1973 and was the longest serving President of the party. Hemant is now Working President and the youngest CM of the state. He was elevated to President on 15 April 2025.

Before the 2024 State Assembly Polls, he was arrested in a money laundering case and later released by the High Court.

JMM, whose battle for a separate state fructified in the year 2000, however had to ally with the Congress or the BJP for political gains.

It was only in 2019, that JMM under Hemant's leadership, won an absolute majority, a feat that was repeated in 2024.

A lawyer by profession, Hemant entered politics in 1994 and became an MLA in 2005.

Most of the young dynasts are active on social media. They have grown up as an internet generation and are comfortable with this medium. Thus, they tweet, post on Instagram with millions of their followers watching their every action and decision.

By now, they all know public connect is the essence of success—not the legacy they inherited.

Interestingly, only Akash, Tejashwi Yadav and Chirag Paswan are relatively 'young' among the new lot.

The others have entered their fifties or are almost there. It is just that they are younger than the old politicians who have been around since several decades.

Chapter 7

The Shining Southern Stars

The three clear superheroes of the 2024 General Elections in the Southern Zone were Tamil Nadu Chief Minister and DMK President Muthuvel Karunanidhi Stalin, now seventy-two, former Andhra Pradesh Chief Minister and TDP President Nara Chandrababu Naidu (seventy-four) and Jansena Party founder President Konidela Pawan Kalyan, who is fifty-four.

The formidable captains, Stalin and Naidu-Kalyan combine had meticulously strategised fail-safe victory plans for their respective states, Tamil Nadu and Andhra Pradesh. And, while they were leading their parties with a missionary zeal, two young lieutenants were working tirelessly to translate their brilliant poll plans into achievable victories.

In the process, forty-seven-year-old Udhayanidhi Stalin, and Nara Lokesh, forty-one, sons of MK Stalin and Chandrababu Naidu re-established their claims on their political legacies, the DMK and the TDP. There were no doubts here, and no dispute!

DMK-led I.N.D.I.A swept the polls in Tamil Nadu winning all the thirty-nine Lok Sabha seats, decimating AIADMK and dashing the BJP's dreams of expanding its footprints in the state, which has so far witnessed two-way electoral battles between the two regional forces after the Congress dominance ended in the 1960s.

Since 1967, the DMK and the AIADMK have dictated the politics of the largest state in the Southern zone, compelling both the national parties, the Congress and the BJP, to ally with either of them in the elections.

The scenario is unlikely to change soon!

Ahead of the 2024 elections, an ambitious BJP saw an opportunity to seize the title of the main opposition party in the state from the AIADMK, which had weakened after the death of its leader, J Jayalalithaa in 2016. However, that wasn't to be. AIADMK retained the title of principal opposition by independently polling 20.26 per cent votes, while the BJP could manage only 11.24 per cent.

Caste coalitions were built by all the three political combinations led by DMK, BJP and AIADMK.

DMK, which led I.N.D.I.A, secured 46.97 per cent votes (DMK alone got 26.93 per cent). AIADMK stood second with 23.05 per cent votes and NDA was at 18.28 per cent. However, BJP's hard work did turn the contest triangular in a hitherto bi-polar state.

In Andhra Pradesh, which was the second largest state in the South till its bifurcation in 2014, the TDP faced a tougher challenge in an election which was critical for its leader Chandrababu Naidu's political future. He was staring at a blank wall when the elections were announced. TDP was wobbling at twenty-three seats in an Assembly of 175 and just three seats out of twenty-five in the Lok Sabha. Naidu had been incarcerated in a corruption case.

TDP needed an ally to bolster its electoral prospects but

Naidu, a poll technician, remained non-committal on his potential poll partner. And there was a reason. The BJP's strongman Amit Shah had permanently closed the NDA's doors for TDP in 2019 after Naidu had withdrawn his ministers from the coalition government and staged a day-long dharna in Delhi over the contentious issue of special status to Andhra Pradesh, an issue that is hanging fire till date. An insightful Naidu forced open the same doors that were slammed on him.

The Janasena Party leader Pawan Kalyan, a time-tested ally of the BJP, proved to be his trump card. Pawan played Pied Piper in bringing the TDP and the BJP together. He met Naidu at the Rajamahendravaram Central Prison on 14 September 2023, about eight months before simultaneous polls to the Lok Sabha and State Assembly were announced. He was accompanied by Naidu's son and TDP General Secretary Nara Lokesh and lawmaker Nandamuri Balakrishna. Their meeting created ripples in political circles.

Naidu was arrested on corruption charges at the behest of the then Chief Minister and Yuvajana Sramika Rythu Congress Party (YSRCP) President Jagan Mohan Reddy, but the High Court set him free after fifty-three days of imprisonment. His arrest generated a wave of sympathy, which he tactfully converted into votes after forging an alliance with formidable allies.

'It made me stronger and more determined to work for the people who stood by me during those distressing days in jail,' Naidu had said at the *Hindustan Times* Summit in Delhi after becoming CM.

Immediately after his release, Naidu started implementing the blueprint he had drawn in jail. The first of his multi-pronged strategy was to motivate cadres and middle-rung leaders with whom he had always maintained an emotional connect.

Experts were roped in and a consultancy company was hired to plan out an elaborate state-wide campaign, but the poll strategy was drawn by Naidu himself.

Naidu had been a master strategist for his father-in-law, popular film star and founder President of the TDP, NT Rama Rao, also a three-time AP Chief Minister.

Brand Naidu dwarfed his rivals as after building social alliances, he had zealously launched public campaigns to expose CM Jagan Mohan Reddy through his selfie campaign, roadshows and public meetings.

The coalition led by TDP with BJP and Janasena Party as poll partners bounced back in the elections reversing his 2019 humiliating defeat into a spectacular victory. The coalition won twenty-one out of twenty-five Lok Sabha seats, polling 53.37 per cent votes, and 164 out of 175 assembly seats. The incumbent YSRCP barely won four seats in the Lok Sabha and eleven seats in the Vidhan Sabha polls. Congress-led I.N.D.I.A failed to even open its account in both the assembly and Lok Sabha polls.

The YSRCP had accomplished a similar feat, winning 151 of the 175 assembly seats and twenty-two of the twenty-five Lok Sabha seats in the previous elections.

Naidu became CM for the fourth time and a kingmaker at the Centre. All through, his son Lokesh played a crucial role in connecting with the youth and manning the central command office and the war rooms. Lokesh was rewarded as he now occupies the chair of the deputy Chief Minister.

> After the failure of his robust welfare agenda, YS Jagan Mohan Reddy said in an interview, 'I am shocked to understand what happened to the love and affection showered by 53 lakh mothers who had received Rs 15,000 for a year under the Amma Vodi scheme, one crore self-help group women who received

financial assistance under the Cheyutha scheme and 66 lakh old age people who were given enhanced pension at their doorsteps. Why haven't they voted for our party?' (Srinivasa Rao Apparasu, *Hindustan Times*, 6 June 2024)

Politics is, indeed, a great leveller.

Narendra Modi, the leader of the same mighty NDA, which had permanently closed the party doors on a regional force, the TDP, needed its support to fulfil his dream of becoming the Prime Minister for a consecutive third term. Naidu willingly extended support, but at what price and for how long is everyone's guess.

Naidu had earlier played an important role in the making of three Prime Ministers, Deve Gowda, Inder Kumar Gujral and Atal Bihari Vajpayee, which is a clear reflection of the power regional parties hold in a hung Parliament.

Pawan Kalyan himself had been struggling after the formation of the Janasena Party (JSP) in March 2014. Today, it's the second largest party in the state assembly, which is quite a leap from its maiden 2019 Assembly polls when JSP had won just one seat and secured six per cent votes.

The BJP finally found a foothold in a state which had been inhospitable so far.

Apparently, the national parties would need regional allies in the state, like in Tamil Nadu, to swim through turbulent waters in the elections, the second state out of their reach. The Congress has better electoral prospects as it had last ruled the state from 2004 to 2014 with change in leadership, thrice.

PM Modi had received a warm welcome during his first visit to the state in January 2025. Modi tried to strike a bond with the people, saying the development of AP was their mission and commitment. Naidu had tweeted, thanking the PM for laying the foundations and inaugurations of projects worth Rs two lakh crores.

There are five states in the Southern region of the country. The two other states where the regional parties would remain in play are Telangana and Karnataka. Kerala has long been a Communist stronghold.

K Chandrashekhar Rao, the founder President of Telangana Rashtra Samithi (TRS), renamed as Bharat Rashtra Samithi (BRS) had lost the 2023 Assembly polls and the 2024 General Elections, but he continues to remain a popular figure, which is indicated by the swelling crowds at his rallies in which he brazenly reminds people about their political blunder. The new Congress CM Revanth Reddy will have to deliver on his promises to people to stop Rao from coming back to power.

Rao's confidence of returning to power in the next election is also mirrored in his statement that BRS would prefer to wait for five years, instead of toppling the government as he wanted the people of the state to realise their blunder and demolish the Congress-led government and bring them back to power for 20 years.

Interestingly, CM A Revanth Reddy has been accusing the BRS of plotting a conspiracy to topple his government. Chandrashekhar Rao contends the BJP would not allow the Congress to complete its term.

The people of the youngest state in the country had twice rewarded TRS for its relentless battle for the creation of Telangana.

TRS had won both the 2014 and 2018 Assembly polls. He became first CM of the state and won a second term, too. The Praja Kutami (People's Alliance) led by the Congress and comprising TDP and CPI had failed to defeat the Father of Telangana, a sobriquet earned by Rao, in the 2018 Assembly polls. The BJP with its skimpy infrastructure had won only one seat then.

However, after his second win, Rao grew ambitious and in his quest for a national role renamed TRS as BRS, but had lost both the polls, that too when the state was celebrating ten years of its formation.

The Congress pushed its way forward in the 2023 Assembly elections and along with the CPI won sixty-five seats while the BRS tally fell to thirty-nine. The BJP in alliance with the Janasena Party contested 111 and 8 seats respectively. The BJP won 8 seats while JSA ended in a zero. TDP had not contested the polls.

BRS failed to win a single seat in the 2024 Lok Sabha elections with the Congress and the BJP sharing eight seats each and AIMIM winning one.

There are seventeen Lok Sabha seats in the state. Today, when Narendra Modi is heading a minority government, Rao has no voice in Parliament. So much for his national role.

Apparently, the contest for Telangana would remain between BRS and Congress. Rao is banking on the growing anti-incumbency against the Congress government in the state. His tacit understanding with the BJP is no more a secret.

Unlike BRS which is holding on to its ground, the JD(S) the main regional player in Karnataka, a state infamous for scams and scandals, desertions and divisions, has been on a downslide.

Karnataka, earlier known as Mysore, was ruled by the Congress from 1947 to 1983, when for the first time, Rama Krishna Hegde of Janata Party had become CM. Thereafter, Janata Dal and Congress rotated power.

The BJP had come in the picture for the first time in 2008, when it emerged as the single largest party. BS Yediyurappa was sworn in as CM. However, he resigned after two days without facing the trust vote, throwing cold water on the political ambitions of the BJP, as it was its maiden government in the South. Thus, the BJP did not relent on its claim.

JD(S), founded in 1999, had given the country its eleventh Prime Minister Deve Gowda for ten months and ruled the state twice for one year and 247 days in 2006-07 and one year and sixty-four days in 2018.

Here is how: The 2004 Assembly polls had thrown a hung house in which JD(S) had emerged as a kingmaker. The Congress-JD(S) formed a coalition government which lasted till 2006.

It was *Kissa Badi Kursi Ka* (a fight for the bigger chair), as JD(S) wanted the CM's throne occupied by the Congress and withdrew from the coalition.

The JD(S) struck a deal with the BJP and formed a coalition government under a power sharing arrangement in which the JD(S) leader HD Kumaraswamy got the first term of twenty months, thereafter which he had to hand over the baton to the BJP. The government fell in 2007, as he refused to stick to the agreement.

The state came under President's Rule and went for assembly polls in 2008, in which the BJP leader and CM-in-waiting YS Yediyurappa's played victim card and won 110 seats, still short of a majority in a house of 224.

JD(S) was rejected by the people, but with twenty-eight seats in its kitty fired a coalition drama. The BJP formed the government and completed its term with three changes in the leadership, amid charges of corruption.

The 2013 Assembly polls gave a clear majority to the Congress, but the 2018 Assembly polls again threw a hung house. JD(S) with thirty-seven seats had enough room to play kingmaker. The five-year term was ruled either by BJP or JD(S).

Now, both the national parties are well-settled in the state.

The Congress is in power since May 2023 prior to which the BJP ruled the state from 2019-2023.

The role of the JD(S) is limited to hung houses or coalitions, as in its present debilitated state, the party cannot win a majority on its own.

Kerala has been a stronghold of national parties—the Congress and the Communists. It also opened its doors for the BJP for the first time in the 2024 Lok Sabha elections.

Sixty-five-year-old BJP leader Suresh Gopi won the Thrissur Lok Sabha seat in 2024, after facing two defeats in 2019 Lok Sabha and 2021 Vidhan Sabha elections. The win came after an extensive voter outreach programme of the BJP led by Gopi, a tinsel town star.

Suresh Gopi, an action hero of Malayalam cinema, had joined BJP in 2016. He was elected to the Rajya Sabha with a task to build the BJP in an inaccessible state. He is now a minister in Modi 3.0.

He had started his career in films as a child artist. He starred in more than 250 films.

Finally with a foothold in the state, the BJP is now preparing for the 2026 Assembly polls. However, here the fight is between national parties and not with a regional force.

The BJP had launched its focus on the Southern region, after its flop show there in the 2019 Lok Sabha elections. It had also realised the need to dispel its image of a Northern party, just as it had removed the upper caste tag in the Northern states. Modi did not have the same traction in the South as in the North.

Besides Modi's extensive campaign in the region, the BJP had also developed local leadership, mellowed down its Hindu-Hindi image and had reached out to various castes in a bid to force triangular contests in states, dominated by regional parties.

Successors and stars

A crop of young dynamic stars including some dynasts have appeared on the big political screen in the South. They are poised to play an impactful role in three of the five southern states—in Tamil Nadu, Andhra Pradesh and Telangana.

BRS President K Chandrashekhar Rao (KCR) has not as yet defined his succession line, while TDP leader Chandrababu Naidu is silent on the growing perception about his son Lokesh, inheriting his mantle. However, there is unlikely to be any dissent or drama, either in public or in the family, after the party supremos decide and declare a successor. Lokesh is national general secretary of TDP. KT Rama Rao and Joginapally Santosh Kumar, son and nephew of KCR, are holding the prime positions of working president and general secretary in the party.

Only the DMK President Stalin has rolled out his succession plan.

Udhayanidhi Stalin of DMK

Forty-seven-year-old Udhayanidhi Stalin is a film actor, producer and distributor and is now also a full-time politician. His father MK Stalin is grooming him to inherit the DMK.

Udhayanidhi had also taken the film route to establish himself in politics, using the silver screen to create his public image, just as his grandfather Karunanidhi and father MK Stalin had done. Interestingly, Stalin had acted in films that were written by his father, but he became more successful in politics than films. Films have been an essential ingredient in the making of politicians in Tamil Nadu.

A politically suave Karunanidhi, heading a huge family, had started implementing his succession plan five years before his death in 2018.

Slowly and steadily, Karunanidhi had groomed Stalin, who is often described as the longest serving political apprentice in the country.

It had taken Stalin twelve years to be elevated as CM after becoming deputy CM in 2009, when with the help of his father, he had honed his administrative skills under the guidance of able bureaucrats. He became working president of the DMK close to his father's death and CM in 2021.

Stalin is now using his father's bluebook to groom Udhayanidhi, but has fast-tracked the process. Udhayanidhi entered politics in 2019, became an MLA in 2021 and minister in 2022; he was elevated to the deputy CM post in 2024.

As a part of his grooming, Stalin frequently sends him for important political functions outside the state so that he can network and build political relations across party lines. Udhayanidhi is interactive and decisive in his official meetings and while addressing crowds, he is decidedly witty.

> At a recent gathering to celebrate Udhayanidhi's forty-seventh birthday, Anbil Mahesh Poyyamozhi, (the education minister) had exclaimed to cheering cadres, '*Indraya* Deputy CM, *Oru naal* definitely CM" (Today's deputy CM is tomorrow's definite CM).' (*PTI*, 26 November 2024)

There were other remarks, too.

> It is no longer a race; but a coronation-in-waiting. The crown, however, comes with thorns of nepotism—one more than his father wore. As he gets battle-ready, taking aim from the enemy lines are some young guns such as TVK Vijay and BJP's K Annamalai.' (Julie Mariappan, *Times of India*, 10 December 2024)

His father Stalin had faced opposition from within the family with his elder brother MK Alagiri opposing the decision tooth and nail even after their father Kurunanidhi had announced his preference. Alagiri was suspended from the party, but he kept firing salvos from his home district Madurai. A day after Karunanidh's death in 2018, Alagiri had again staked his claim but did not get the party's support.

Udhayanidhi visited his estranged uncle Alagiri in January 2023. They said it was a family meet while some experts described it as a shrewd move on Udhayanidhi's part. Senior political analyst, RK Radhakrishnan had this to say:

> Udhayanidhi Stalin is an extremely clever operator who is trying to secure his position within the family. The first thing that anybody needs to do within Karunanidhi's extended family is to secure their position within. Udhayanidhi wants Alagiri's support within the family.'

Both father and son have been aggressively countering BJP's subtle moves to impose Hindi and Hindutva, a contentious issue in the entire South.

In September 2023, Udhayanidhi had made a scathing attack on Sanatan Dharma and while comparing it with dengue and malaria had called for its eradication. The AIADMK and BJP leaders were livid and had demanded an apology from him.

However, he had fiercely defended his statement, saying he had only spoken the party's ideology and invoked the names of iconic figures of the South, BR Ambedkar, EV Ramasamy aka Periyar and Thirumavalavan.

It was a calculated move, emphasising a mix of emotional, religious, linguistic and welfare issues at a time when the BJP is trying to entice Tamilians with temple politics.

The Modi government had launched the annual month-long Kashi Tamil Sangamam in 2022. It's a cultural initiative of the Centre aimed at rediscovering the historical and cultural connection between Kashi and Tamil Nadu. At its third edition in 2025, the Centre honoured the state's most revered figure Agasthiyar Munivar for his contribution to the literature, language and culture of Tamil Nadu. Kashi is the Lok Sabha constituency of Prime Minister Narendra Modi.

DMK is aware of the subtle moves of the BJP-ruled Central Government. Thus, while opposing the draft recommendations of the University Grants Commission (UGC), MK Stalin had vowed to oppose the three-language policy and the National Education Policy to protect Tamil identity. He had described it as a blatant attempt to impose Hindi and Sanskrit on non-Hindi speaking states. He had also led the southern states in their fight against population-based delimitation in 2026 to preserve their political power, relevance and voice. As compared to the North, the states in the South have proactively worked to contain their population and they thus fear weakening of their presence in Parliament.

Senior journalist and content creator Lakshmana Kuchi says Tamilians don't fall for Hindutva. They revere Ram and Shiva, but they also have their own deities.

Udhayanidhi's major challenge would be the 2026 Tamil Nadu Assembly elections in which the superstar Vijay Thalapathy will make his electoral debut. Tamil pride will be the slogan.

KT Rama Rao of BRS

Although Kalvakuntla Taraka Rama Rao, who is forty-eight is today the working president of BRS, he can't be sure about inheriting his father's legacy.

His father and founder president of the TRS, K Chandrashekhar Rao has not as yet shared his mind with anyone—neither with the family nor senior party leaders—on his successor. And no one has the courage to ask him.

According to a senior journalist from *The Hindu*, Abhinay Deshpande, the primary contenders of his legacy are his son KTR, his daughter K Kavitha and his nephew T Harish Rao. All three have made significant contributions to the party and state politics. During his tenure as CM, KCR had promoted his son KTR, creating an impression he was the de facto leader.

Interestingly, when KCR was planning to assume a national role to expand BRS or lead the Third Front of the non-BJP and non-Congress parties, many had expected to see KTR in the CM's role. It did not happen and after losing the 2024 Lok Sabha polls, KCR has also lost the kingmaker's position to Naidu. KCR is now spending most of his time at his farm, while KTR occupies the opposition benches in the state assembly.

KTR, as working president of BRS (earlier known as TRS) and a minister in the Rao government, had played a significant role in evolving the party's organisational strategy as well as in the governance of the state, particularly in the Information Technology department and Municipal Administration. However, his immediate elevation to the party president's post seems unlikely, though the cadre looks upon him as KCR's successor.

Kavitha, a former MP and now an MLA is also active in mobilising support of women, while T Harish Rao is a seasoned politician known for his administrative and political acumen. He is a seven-time MLA.

The two front runners for Rao's legacy are KTR and Harish Rao—the former is perceived as an urban leader and the latter as a mass leader.

The suspense of who will wear the crown will remain till KCR delivers his verdict. He is known for making strategic decisions well in advance and revealing them only at an opportune time. He knows his decision would be binding on the party and people, and that the family will accept his wisdom. Any infighting and division in the family is ruled out, as the glue that would keep them united is business, besides their passion for politics.

KCR and his successor have a gigantic task to win the 2028 assembly polls for them to return to power and for their party to revive and thrive.

Nara Lokesh (Andhra Pradesh)

Forty-one-year-old Nara Lokesh, an MBA from the Stanford Graduate School of Business and Bachelor of Science with a specialisation in Management Information Systems from Carnegie Mellon University was considered to be an obvious choice for TDP's Presidentship, as and when Naidu decided to relinquish the position.

Interestingly while Naidu has been ahead of leaders of his generation in technology-driven innovative ideas, Lokesh's mantra is also 'leveraging technology to drive development and prosperity of Andhra Pradesh,' according to his LinkedIn profile as Minister of IT, Electronics and Communications, Human Resources Development. In a run up to the elections, Lokesh had taken out a *Yuva Galam Padayatra* for 400 days to connect with the youth of the state.

Lokesh would be the third-generation leader to head TDP, which was founded by his grandfather NT Rama Rao. He doesn't have many competitors in the family vying for the coveted post.

The Naidu family is too interwoven to bear a messy transition and after his return to power, the voice of Chandrababu Naidu would prevail, in their powerful and united Kamma community, the big family and the party.

However, Naidu has to decide and declare his successor, though he himself had to grab the party and the position from his father-in-law in a coup.

It may be recalled, Naidu had joined the Indian Youth Congress in 1975. He was elected to the state assembly in 1978 and became minister in 1980. Naidu was given several portfolios including cinematography. He came in touch with NT Rama Rao, a popular actor, director of Telugu cinema and married his daughter, Nara Bhuvaneswari in 1981.

NT Rama Rao had launched TDP in 1982 which swept its maiden assembly election in 1983. Naidu, however, had continued with the Congress till he lost the election to a TDP candidate.

Naidu quit the Congress and joined the TDP. He started building the party, which was still in a nascent stage. He became party general secretary in 1986, and party coordinator in 1989. He started organising training camps for party leaders. A subtle messaging was done about him taking over the TDP through these camps. In 1994, Naidu became the finance minister in the NT Rama Rao government. At the party level, NT Rama Rao kept delaying his appointment as secretary-general lest he get blamed for promoting nepotism. Eventually, Naidu staged a coup against his father-in-law and became CM in 1995.

Circa 1990 when the TDP had lost power in the state to the Congress.

> Around that time NTR, a widower, remarried. His new bride, much younger than him, started wielding tremendous influence within the party. This was not taken kindly by NTR's children, and certainly not by his son-in-law Naidu. In 1995,

> Naidu staged a coup to oust NTR in a leading hostel where he collected TDP MLAs. Most MLAs sided with Naidu and NTR was deposed and his son-in-law soon took control of the party and later the government.
>
> (Kingshuk Nag, *Deccan Herald*, 10 June 2024)

A visionary, Naidu never looked back and built Cyberabad, an IT city, which won him as well as his party, accolades. Now he is building his dream project Amravati, the state capital as a modern and bustling city.

Now, Lokesh is married to Brahmani Nara, daughter of NT Rama Rao's sixth son Nandamuri Balakrishna, actor-cum-politician. He has represented the Hindupur Assembly constituency since 2014 and could have been a claimant against Nara Lokesh, but people say he would not upset the applecart for family reasons.

Thus, Nara Lokesh, who often describes himself as a *karyakarta* (worker) would have smooth sailing and may perhaps require his wife's political wisdom to pull out strategies as sharp as the ones built by Naidu. Would she come out and play an active role? So far, women have not publicly played a key role in TDP politics.

Nara became minister for the first time in 2017, but he lost the Assembly elections in 2019 and later won it in 2024. He is currently a cabinet minister holding charge of IT, Electronics, Communications and Human Resources Development in his father's government.

Nara Lokesh would inherit a strong party infrastructure, but he is not a patch on his father's political skills and acumen. The next elections are five years away, but continuing the alliance with the BJP may turn out to be a rollercoaster ride. Public expectations are huge from the TDP government, as Naidu is called the development icon.

Pawan Kalyan had lived up to his name and done their *kalyan* in 2024!

He, who has been a consistent ally of the BJP had fixed and forged a three-party alliance to take on YSRCP.

Pawan Kalyan

Fifty-three-year-old Pawan Kalyan is a Telugu actor and is also known as Power Star. He is also Chiranjeevi's brother.

He founded the Janasena Party (JSP) in 2014. The party registered its electoral presence in its first 2019 Assembly polls winning one of the 137 seats it had contested. Kalyan himself fought from two seats and lost both.

Till the 2024 polls, Pawan Kalyan had no political achievement to flaunt or showcase, besides his on-screen personality that made him one of the leading actors of Telugu cinema.

Even after failing in the 2019 polls, Pawan had not given up on his efforts. He started courting the BJP and befriended TDP while strengthening his party.

A popular action hero, Pawan also brought much of his screen play onto the streets, using his flamboyance to attract crowds like walking around all in white on the beach in Visakhapatnam to raise the issue of violation of building construction norms in the region.

He launched the Janavani programme to hold small interactive sessions with the public. He invited the CM's wrath, but established himself in the political world.

A fiery speaker, Pawan used to drive his fans into a frenzy by his theatrical acts, like symbolically taking off his slippers to whip the CM's effigy for calling him 'package star,' as he was working for the BJP and TDP.

Pawan had been advocating for the opposition's unity against the YSRCP government, but the BJP was playing truant while TDP was sceptical. He managed to persuade them and pushed them onto the negotiating table. The turning point was Babu's arrest by the YSRCP government.

He had earlier lived in the shadow of his superstar brother Chiranjeevi, supporting his political venture, Praja Rajyam, founded in 2008. Chiranjeevi returned to cinema, merging his party with the Congress. Pawan launched JSP in March 2014.

A decade later, his efforts paid huge results as the TDP-BJP-Janasena coalition won the Lok Sabha and Assembly elections infusing fresh life into the TDP, the BJP as well as JSP. It became the second largest party in the state and he became Deputy CM.

Pawan is a go-getter, but he has been playing his cards cautiously, perhaps knowing that he is caught between two mavericks—Chandrababu Naidu and Narendra Modi.

His future depends on his performance as Deputy CM, as there is no scope for flops in the political theatre and histrionics are not of much help in governance.

Pawan has embraced Hindutva and emerged as a protector of Sanatan Dharma in the South. The TDP espouses secularism. It could be Sanatan vs Secularism as and when they would have an ideological clash. Though the TDP government would survive, the NDA government is likely to collapse as breaking the TDP is not a viable option before the BJP high command. Right now, Pawan stands between the two formidable allies, each smarter than the other.

Can his *aandhi* (storm), as Prime Minister Narendra Modi had described him, really turn the tide in his favour or would the BJP adopt him?

People believe JSP would survive as Pawan Kalyan is a horse ready for a long race.

Joseph Vijay Chandrasekhar (Tamil Nadu)

Cinema has produced many successful political stars in Tamil Nadu, as they carefully selected their roles to build their public persona, unlike Bollywood in which even the tallest and most versatile actor, Amitabh Bachchan had failed to shine in the political arena. Bachchan was elected from Allahabad in the 1984 Lok Sabha elections. He had emerged as a giant killer after defeating political stalwart Hemvati Nandan Bahuguna.

The new entrant, Vijay at fifty, picked up the same tinsel route to create waves on the political screen with his fan clubs turning into his party cadres.

Vijay floated the Tamilaga Vettri Kazhagam (TVK) in 2024 with a declared ideology of secularism and social justice. At his first public meeting, Vijay maintained an equal distance from both the BJP and the DMK, describing the saffron party as an ideological enemy and the DMK, as their political enemy. Garlanding pictures and statues of former Congress leader Kamaraj along with other iconic and ideological figures like Periyar and Ambedkar at his party's public functions had raised questions about his potential affiliations with the grand old party in the 2026 Assembly polls.

Before launching the party, Vijay had tested the waters in 2011 when his fan club, Vijay Makkal Iyakkham, formed in 2009, had supported the AIADMK in the assembly polls and had contested the 2021 local bodies elections in the state. Their performance had given him the courage to take the plunge into politics.

He is popular but will need a natural inclination for politics to establish his fledgling regional party. His political choices and moves would translate his silver screen fans into votes. As of now, he is creating the same excitement in politics that a film generates before its release.

Annamalai Kuppusamy

On 27 December 2024, the 40-year-old BJP state president was seen whipping himself to protest against the DMK government for its inaction over a sexual assault case in Anna University in Tamil Nadu. A day earlier, Anna had announced he would not wear footwear till DMK was ousted from power.

A management graduate from IIM Lucknow, Anna is an IPS officer of the 2011 batch. He was posted as Deputy Commissioner in South Bengaluru and had earned the reputation of a Singham (tough cop) before joining the BJP in 2020. He lost elections he had contested in 2021 and again in 2024.

In Tamil Nadu, where films have played a vital role in building political careers, Anna a real-time Singham has been tasked to defeat the mighty DMK and AIADMK too, if not in an alliance. So far, both the BJP and the AIADMK have been giving conflicting signals.

The BJP was relying on Anna, a star whose dramatics on streets outshines the screen performances of cine stars till they opened doors for AIADMK, whose general secretary, Edappadi K Palaniswami met Amit Shah in Delhi on 25 March 2025. Since then, he has been lying low while displaying his discomfort with the emerging alliance. He is the man to watch!

Why regional parties dominate

Regional parties have dominated the Southern states and film stars their politics in two of the five states, Tamil Nadu and Andhra

Pradesh. They had also dominated Karnataka and Telangana.

Southern India comprises five states with a total of 131 of the 543 Lok Sabha seats spread out as follows: Tamil Nadu (thirty-nine), Karnataka (twenty-eight), Andhra Pradesh (twenty-one) Kerala (sixteen) and Telangana (sixteen).

The national parties had found suitable partners in the 2024 polls. The BJP allied with the TDP and Janasena Party in Andhra Pradesh, Janata Dal(S) in Karnataka, smaller parties in Tamil Nadu and Kerala, but with none in Telangana.

Similarly, the Congress had stitched alliances with DMK and others in Tamil Nadu, smaller parties besides Communists in Kerala, but with none in the other three states. In all, regional forces won fifty-five seats irrespective of their alliances or with no alliance.

While the Congress had ruled these states since Independence till the mid-1960s, Andhra Pradesh had its first non-Congress CM in 1983.

There are two features peculiar to the Southern belt.

First, cinema, as said earlier, continues to play a significant role in building public images of leaders with their fan clubs converting into propaganda machinery at the time of elections. This is more pronounced in Tamil Nadu and in Andhra Pradesh.

Tamil Nadu is the only state in the country to be ruled by a regional party either independently or in alliance with the national parties since 1967. Only two CMs did not have a film background.

Second, the regional parties have protected their turf while maintaining cordial relations with the Central Government, irrespective of its colour or ideology. The interest of the state and their party is paramount.

> The Dravida movement was centred on the Tamil language, Tamil culture and an idea of a Tamil nation which opposed anything nationalistic and Indian. To temper the demand for a separate Dravida Nadu, business and industrial houses had successfully lobbied with the central government to set up new industries in the state. (*EPW*, What Influences Electoral Politics in Southern India, 3 May 2019)

Karnataka saw unholy alliances, scams and drama by the three players since 2004 till the people had started delivering a clear mandate.

JD(S) was born in 1999 and its intemperate behaviour explains the unethical roles that regional parties sometimes play for their political growth, often blackmailing and bargaining for positions and posts. They dump pre-poll allies for favours.

In Andhra Pradesh, the TDP founder NT Rama Rao had famously said 'TDP came with me and will go away with me.' As the Congress failed to fulfil the regional aspirations of the people, the TDP under Naidu became a viable alternative.

Founder Director of C voter, Yashwant Deshmukh commenting on the North vs South debate said that the South of Vindhyas has been dumping the BJP, but the fact of the matter is the BJP is as strong as the Congress or the Congress is as weak as the BJP in the South.

Deshmukh suggested a study of the assembly poll results in Tamil Nadu where the BJP alliance polled 18 per cent, almost at par with the AIADMK (21 per cent). The Congress is nowhere close to the DMK, its Lok Sabha partner. The possibility of the BJP overtaking the Congress in the South cannot be ruled out.

On the future of regional parties in the South, Deshmukh had a different take. 'They are waning in Telangana and Karnataka which may see bi-polar elections between the national parties in the next few years.'

However, my assessment is that Telangana may still slip from the grip of the national parties, as the regional aspirations are huge. Regional parties will continue to dominate the politics of Andhra Pradesh and Tamil Nadu as of now.

There are other issues too!

In 2024, some Southern leaders had raised objections over the fall in their share in Central taxes, noting how for the last thirty years, tax devolution had been increasing for Northern states and decreasing for South.

This was not the first time when the burning issue of the Centre's discrimination was collectively raised. The MPs from South, individually or collectively, have been meeting Central leaders with their demands for better share to Southern states.

Senior journalist Lakshmana Kuchi attributes the dominance of regional parties in the South to the failure of the national parties to respect the aspirations and culture of the region.

South India is relatively more educated and aware of ground realities, including the role played by the national parties and the contribution of the regional parties in the development of the region and protection of their identity.

Late UP chief minister, Narain Dutt Tiwari, who had held important portfolios like Finance and Industry in the Central Government used to laud unity in the Southern states in pushing their economic agenda, notwithstanding their disputes over water and rivers.

They fought the Centre for their state's development, but without yielding political space to the parties in power at the Centre, a blunder committed by the regional forces in the North.

Chapter 8

The Legacy on the Brink

Papa Meri Jaan, Hardam Rakhna Ab Haath Yeh Sar Par Tum,
Papa Meri Jaan, Mere Sang Chalna Har Meel Ka Pathar Tum,
Tumhi Pe Toh Theherte Hai, Yeh Raaste Mere, Papa Meri Jaan.

While fighting several severe political battles without his father's protective shield, Sukhbir Singh Badal, the sixty-two-year-old beleaguered leader of the country's oldest regional party, the Shiromani Akali Dal (SAD), can feel and fathom the emotional lyrics of the song sung by Sonu Nigam in Ranbir Kapoor's film *Animal*. Sukhbir knows he desperately needs his father's skills and shrewdness to come out of the crisis, unscathed.

On 3 December 2024, Sukhbir looked pensive while sitting on a wheelchair with his fractured foot, performing the duties of a *sevadaar* (volunteer) at the entrance of the Golden Temple in Amritsar. The former deputy chief minister of Punjab was dressed in a blue robe carrying a spear such as that carried by the guards on duty. A placard with a hymn from the Gurbani, was hung around his neck.

Sukhbir was offering penance for 'religious misconduct,' on the *Hukumnama* (diktat) of the Akal Takht, the highest temporal body of the Sikhs during which he also braved an assassination attempt on himself. The world watched the developments with utmost curiosity.

The Akal Takht, established by the sixth Sikh guru Hargobind Singh in the seventeenth century, accepts petitions and takes decisions pertaining to the Sikh community; their orders are binding on all, irrespective of their status in society. SAD rebels had earlier lodged a complaint about Sukhbir's abject failures on many fronts, including the representation of Sikhs' interests while in power.

Invoking the centuries-old tradition, the Akal Takht on 30 August 2024 had declared Sukhbir and others in the party and the government, *tankhaiya*—guilty of religious misconduct—for the decisions he had taken between 2007-2017, as deputy CM. His father, the SAD President late Parkash Singh Badal was then the Chief Minister.

'Being the deputy CM of Punjab and President of the Shiromani Akali Dal, Sukhbir Singh Badal took such decisions that deeply harmed the image of the Panth and greatly weakened the SAD. This has damaged the interests of Sikhs, too,' Jathedar Giani Raghbir Singh had said while pronouncing the verdict in the Golden Temple complex. The media had reported it extensively.

Sukhbir along with his ministers were directed to appear at the Akal Takht in person and submit their written explanations within fifteen days.

The allegations against him included pardoning of Dera Sachcha Sauda chief Gurmeet Ram Rahim in the 2007 blasphemy case and the state government's failure to punish the perpetrators of the Bargari sacrilege case—the desecration of the Sikh holy book, the *Guru Granth Sahib* in a gurudwara in Bangari village in Faridkot in 2015.

In a pre-emptive move, Sukhbir in December 2023 had apologised to the Sikh community for his failure to arrest the culprits in the Bargari sacrilege case. Much earlier, Parkash Singh Badal had also written an emotional letter to the Akal Takht Jathedar after paying obeisance at the Golden Temple. He had written, 'I share my pain and anguish over the incident and have reached here to pray before the *Wahe Guru* to give me strength and blessings.'

Yet the incident returned to haunt his son Sukhbir in August 2024.

Jathedar Giani Raghbir Singh said, 'Until Sukhbir Singh Badal appears before the Takht Sahib as a humble Sikh in the presence of *Guru Granth Sahib, Sikh Sangat* and *Panj Singh Sahiban* to apologise for his offences, he is being declared *tankhaiya* (guilty of religious misconduct).'

Immediately, Sukhbir had tweeted that he bows his head before the highest temporal seat and would soon present himself before Shri Akal Takht Sahib to seek forgiveness.

> In a video message, SAD vice-president Daljit Singh Cheema had said that the party bows before the edict and would act accordingly. He said, 'Sukhbir Singh Badal had appeared before Akal Takht last month and accepted his government's mistakes and also announced that the orders of the supreme temporal seat would be followed in true spirit.' (*Hindustan Times*, 31 August 2024)

A day before he was declared *tankhaiya*, Sukhbir had resigned from the presidentship of SAD and appointed senior leader Balwinder Singh Bhundar as working president. The Akal Takht had directed the party's working committee on 2 December

2024 to accept the resignation within three days and reorganise the party within six months.

After much delay, the working committee of SAD accepted Sukhbir's resignation at its meeting held on 10 January 2025 to quieten dissenting voices. The Akal Takht pardoned him for his religious misconduct in December 2024, accepting his letter seeking forgiveness.

This was not the first time when the Akal Takht had declared a senior political leader as a *tankhaiya.* Many prominent Sikh leaders, including the first Sikh emperor Maharaja Ranjit Singh, former President Giani Jail Singh and former Punjab CM Surjit Singh Barnala had been declared sinners.

Ramesh Vinayak, executive editor of the *Hindustan Times* in Chandigarh said the religious punishment to Sukhbir would lead to a closure of an emotive issue that has been tormenting him and his party since 2016, and eroding its support base in the Panthic constituency.

Sukhbir's ordeals, however, are far from over. He now faces another challenge and this time to the political legacy he had comfortably inherited from his father, the legendary Parkash Singh Badal. While pronouncing the religious punishment, the Akal Takht had also spelled out a 'political prescription' for SAD, which was facing internecine troubles.

A six-member committee, headed by the Shiromani Gurdwara Parbandhak Committee (SGPC) Chairman Harjinder Singh Dhami was constituted to conduct elections of the new party president and executive after holding a fresh membership drive in the state. The time given for the task was six months.

The SGPC, founded in 1920, is an apex governing body of all the gurdwaras in India and abroad and works under the directives of the Akal Takht.

SAD leader Harjinder Singh Dhami was elected President of the SGPC for the fourth term with an overwhelming majority in the annual presidential elections held in October 2024.

There have been controversies about SGPC working under the shadows of SAD.

> Ever since the reins of the Shiromani Akali Dal went to Parkash Singh Badal in 1996, the party's control over Sikh and gurdwara politics from the SGPC platform remained undisputed amid several controversies. Around two decades ago, when Gurcharan Singh Tohra, who headed the SGPC for a record 27 terms passed away, Badal-led-SAD established control over the mini parliament of Sikhs. (GS Paul, *Tribune*, 26 April 2023)

Gurcharan Singh Tohra died in April 2004.

> 'In the various elections to the SGPC, the Akali Dal has managed to get majority seats and, as a result, played a dominant role in electing the SGPC President and Executive body that runs the institution. Leaders also move between SAD and SGPC,' explains Dr Amarjit Singh Narang, author of *Region, Religion and Politics: 100 years of the Shiromani Akali Dal*. (Chitleen K Sethi, *The Print*, 15 September 2024)

Dhami's election against Jagir Kaur, the presidential candidate of SAD (rebel group) must have come as a breather for Sukhbir.

An advocate by profession, Dhami had also appealed to the Sikh community to unite under the leadership of the Akal Takht and as a conciliatory move had withdrawn its petition to the Akal Takht to excommunicate Narain Singh Chaura who had fired at Sukhbir. SAD had also demanded his excommunication amid opposition from some Sikh groups.

> To blunt the controversies plaguing SGPC, Dhami had clarified, 'This 11-member board of Sikh intellectuals will operate under the authority of the Akal Takht, adhering to Sikh '*rehat maryada*' principles. Their primary function will be to address Panthic matters referred to them by the Akal Takht.' (GS Paul, *Tribune*, 1 November 2024)

The SAD election is referred to the SGPC by the Akal Takht. Questions are being raised about the Akal Takht's political intervention, especially in the SAD elections.

> In a secular democracy, where political parties operate within the constitutional framework, however, spiritual authority directly intervening in political decisions could raise questions about the separation of state and religion. (Pramod Kumar, Chairperson, Institute for Development and Communications, Chandigarh, *Indian Express*, 4 December 2024)

Somehow, Punjab politics and religion have been inseparable, though a cocktail of religion and politics is a major issue in the rest of the country, especially after PM Narendra Modi and UP CM Yogi Adityanath have bulldozed their Hindutva agenda since 2014.

A delegation of SAD met Akal Takht Jathedar Giani Raghbir Singh on 9 December 2024 in which it cited the legal hurdles coming in the implementation of its decree on party reorganisation.

Quoting from the Representation of the People Act, 1951, which mandates for running a political party in a secular manner, not as per the directives of a religious body like the Akal Takht, the delegation conveyed its fears of getting derecognised by the Election Commission of India (ECI).

There are innumerable factions of the Akali Dal but the ECI has recognised SAD as a state party. Their fears may not be unfounded after the drama in Maharashtra where the original Shiv Sena and NCP were disrobed of their titles and symbols. SAD and BJP are at loggerheads since the party withdrew from NDA ahead of the General Elections in 2024.

The working committee of the SAD had accepted Sukhbir's resignation on 10 December 2024, almost a month after he had resigned on November 16. The working committee also decided to hold a membership drive from 20 January 2025 and toward culmination of organisational polls with the election for the party president on 1 March 2025.

At a show of strength organised at Maghi Mela in Muktsar on 14 January 2025, Sukhbir struck an emotional chord saying he was willing to sacrifice his life for the *Panth* (Path) and Peace.

The SAD-BSP alliance rally made it clear that there was no challenge from within the party, but from the rebels, as at some distance away from their venue, the rival faction led by jailed Khadoor Sahib MP, Amritpal Singh, a radical preacher and Faridkot MP, Sarabjeet Singh Khalsa, son of one of the assassins of the late Prime Minister Indira Gandhi, had launched a new party, the Shiromani Akali Dal (*Waris Punjab De*) at a parallel show of strength that they had organised. Khalsa said they were forced to launch a new party as Sukhbir Singh Badal had deviated from the path.

A keen observer of Punjab politics, Ramesh Vinayak said it was too early to predict if Sukhbir would redeem himself or would it be the end of the road for him as he is facing challenges from three corners—the clergy, the rebel group and the radicals. However, his instant move to submit himself before the clergy for religious punishment would de-stigmatise Sukhbir and may help him in his political revival. 'It could well be the Akalis' master stroke aimed at blunting the rivals' charges against Sukhbir as well as negating the impression among the Sikh masses about the Badals' stranglehold on the Sikh high priests.'

Sukhbir's emphasis on SAD 'belongs to all and not any one person' was aimed at neutralising the growing criticism about his family's control over the party, and in the process, legitimising his legacy and the party's moderate vision.

Would he get public support with corruption charges tainting the family?

Punjab's legendary figure, Parkash Singh Badal, was born in December 1927 and remained a central figure in Punjab politics for over seven decades.

A freedom fighter, Parkash Singh Badal had seen and survived the country's Partition in 1947, creation of Punjab in its current form in 1966, Indian Emergency in 1977, Sikh extremism and Operation Blue Star in 1984, besides the internal upheavals in the country, his state and in the party.

The longest serving patron of SAD had rubbed shoulders with several Prime Ministers—from Jawaharlal Nehru to Narendra Modi. He died in April 2023 at the age of 95 years. Both SAD and Punjab had faced their first election without their father figure in 2024.

While swimming through turbulent waters, Sukhbir might have realised that inheriting a legacy was easier than surviving or enjoying it. Leading a ship through choppy waters is different from sailing the vessel under someone's care and guidance.

The party was born on 14 December 1920 at the Akal Takht, a month after the formation of SGPC; its mandate was to protect the latter (SGPC) and Gurdwaras. Later, it became a representative political party of the Sikh Community.

> The party's old constitution reads, "Akali Dal's main purpose is to serve Panth, country and the oppressed, to endeavour for improving Gurdwaras management and Sewa".
>
> The words like Panth, Sikh or gurdwaras do not even figure in the 143-word long 'vision and mission' statement and 174-word long note on 'history' of the party's website. These differences between the old and current mission statements underline the gap between the original and current Akali Dal. (IP Singh, *TNN*, 22 May 2023)

Parkash Singh Badal had changed the party's face from Panthic to Punjab. The party website notes, 'The vision of Shiromani Akali Dal is to facilitate attainment of a high quality of life for all citizens of Punjab. This can be attained by establishing peace, tranquility and communal harmony while promoting growth and prosperity. It aims for an educated society imbued with an ambition to prosper; and an economy, which is competitive with sustained growth for the benefit of all. Shiromani Akali Dal is driven by its "Development for All" agenda.' This appeals to all castes and communities in Punjab as well as the youth.

The Akal Takht, which has always played a role of a peacemaker between warring groups to end factionalism in the interests of the party and the community had again given a 'call for unity of brothers' after Sukhbir's atonement for the contentious issues the rebels had been raising. However, the question still remains about the Akal Takht's intervention after SAD's objection to its decree on party organisation. Who would control SAD? Sukhbir is in no mood to concede defeat. This was clear at their Muktsar rally. Sukhbir was unanimously re-elected SAD President on 12 April 2025. In his emotional speech, he promised to never compromise on any issue that could hurt the prestige of the Panth, Punjab and SAD. The rebels were not amused and said his election was a jolt to unity moves.

Continuation of Sukhbir's leadership of a unified party would thus depend on his shrewdness and conciliatory approach in regrouping various factions of the Akali Dal and regaining his credibility in the community to save SAD. It's not always easy to carry forward the political legacy that fathers bestow on their sons.

The people of Punjab often recall the hard work put in by the senior Badal to raise the oldest dynasty in the country. Even after he had crossed into his 90s, he would respond to queries on his age and challenges with, a cryptic, 'Shall run and show.'

It's high time Sukhbir picks up substance along with style. The trek with several expected roadblocks ahead will be lonely!

After the party's flop show in the 2024 General Elections, the voices demanding change in SAD leadership had started getting louder in Punjab. Sukhbir desperately looked for a formula from his father's book, considered a reservoir of experience and knowledge, to mitigate the crisis.

The senior Badal had an illustrious political career. He had started as a sarpanch of his village Badal in 1947 and had won his maiden assembly election from SAD in 1957.

A ten-time member of the Legislative Assembly, five-term longest serving CM of Punjab, three-term leader of opposition in the Punjab Legislative Assembly, besides a stint in the Union Government under Prime Minister Morarji Desai, Parkash Singh Badal was happiest when he was amidst people. He was called the people's politician even by his rivals.

A champion of Sikh-Hindu unity, Badal Senior was an expert in Panthic politics, as well as in building political alliances. A friend of former Prime Minister Atal Bihari Vajpayee, he had steered the BJP-Akali Dal alliance through challenging corridors. He had even made suitable changes in the party's identity.

> Badal had replaced the Panthic agenda with "Punjabiyat," which was acceptable to the moderate Sikhs and the RSS, who believed in "Keshdhari Hindus' ideology". (*abplive.com*)

Political expert Vinod Sharma who has closely seen both senior and junior Badals at work, said: 'Parkash Singh Badal had seen both the pre-Independence and post-Independence era. Prime Minister Narendra Modi had even described him as Nelson Mandela of Punjab as Sr Badal had launched several public movements in the interest of Sikh Panth and spent several years in jail. His politics may have been sectarian but he himself was not parochial. He diligently worked for Hindu-Sikh unity. He had personified Akali Dal but gradually converted the second oldest Indian party, next to Congress, into a family party which penetrated almost all lucrative businesses.'

Senior Badal was honoured with the prestigious Panth Rattan Fakhr-e-Qaum (Jewel of the religion, pride of the community) by the Akal Takht in December 2011, which had evoked much controversy, and a Padma Vibhushan by the President of India in March 2015 for his contribution to politics, agriculture, infrastructure and service to India.

Ironically, when the 2024 General Elections were held in the country almost a year after his death, people fondly remembered the patriarch, but their sentiments or sympathy did not influence the voting pattern in Punjab, even in his ancestral Badal village. SAD had snapped its almost three-decade long alliance with the BJP before the 2024 General Elections, as it did not want the government's farm laws to have a negative impact on its electoral prospects. However, their procrastination in withdrawing the support had hurt the farmers.

In a solo show, SAD could win one seat. Harsimrat Kaur, Sukhbir's wife, retained the Bhatinda seat, which she had won in 2009, 2014 and 2019. A majority of the thirteen candidates lost their security deposits.

Sukhbir had failed to read the public anger on the farm laws and SAD's delayed exit from the NDA. He initially withdrew his wife Harsimrat Kaur from the Modi government and later exited from NDA.

Vinod Sharma, who extensively travelled in Punjab during the elections, however said, 'Akali Dal snapped ties with BJP over farm laws though they together would have performed better in the Lok Sabha elections. But these are the angularities of politics.'

Ahead of the elections, Sukhbir had launched a four-month long *Punjab Bachao Yatra* from February to May 2024, but failed to recuperate the party despite his merciless attack on all the three opposition parties—the BJP for trying to take control of Sikh shrines, the Congress for its anti-Sikh policies and the AAP government for creating a financial mess in the state.

Some political observers were expecting a better performance by SAD in the 2024 elections as Sukhbir was no novice. Parkash Singh Badal, who became SAD's President in 1995 had handed over his legacy to his son in 2008. A pool of senior leaders, groomed by senior Badal, were also guiding him on running the party and fighting the elections. However, nothing helped, not even the sympathy factor.

Now, the family's three-decade long hegemony is in peril. The general perception in Punjab, as echoed by Ramesh Vinayak is, 'When senior Badal was around, it was easier for them to defend their decisions, even brazen them out. But things changed after

2022. They lost their second consecutive assembly elections and then Parkash Singh Badal passed away, leaving behind a weakened Akali Dal' with Sukhbir's at the helm. 'That emboldened the anti-Sukhbir lobby to raise the banner of revolt and take up his and the party's past sins with the clergy.'

Senior Badal had left a rich legacy for his son, but along with a trail of controversies. He was always accused of 'family first' and this had hurt the party most even in the 2017 assembly elections, as in the previous government, the senior Badal had accommodated four family members in his cabinet.

> Today the village, which has been transformed from a dusty hamlet to a sparkling oasis, is eponymous with the first dynasty of Punjab and the Akali Dal. The surname Badal spells power. The Punjab Cabinet has four members of the family—chief minister Badal, his deputy Sukhbir Singh Badal, son-in-law Adesh Partap Singh Kairon and Sukhbir's brother-in-law Bikram Singh Majithia. Sukhbir's wife Harsimrat is a union minister. It's quite a moral climbdown for a leader who was once a harsh critic of the Gandhi dynasty.' (Manraj Grewal Sharma in *Hindustan Times,* 11 December 2016.)

Sukhbir was also the party president. Grewal also quoted Ashutosh Kumar, a Professor at the Political Science Department of Panjab University:

> 'Like Akbar, Badal has used matrimonial alliances to strengthen his hold on Punjab. He married his daughter Parneet into the Congress heavyweight Kairon family, and his son into the powerful Majithia clan. Now he is systematically giving tickets to sons of Akali leaders to promote the hegemony of his own son.'

The senior Badal had always guarded his turf, side-lining potential challengers from within the party and drafting frontline Akali leaders' progeny into Akali politics, all this to consolidate Sukhbir's grip on the party. Grewal continues in the same report:

> In a carefully choreographed succession politics, Sukhbir was anointed party chief, and heir apparent in 2008 when he was barely 45. That laid the foundation of the first family-dominated rule in Akali history. Today, Sukhbir and Harsimrat are the fulcrum of Akali power politics.

Ramesh Vinayak explains further, 'Call it a pull of dynastic politics or a move to outsmart his potential challengers, Parkash Singh Badal appointed Sukhbir as President of SAD in 2008, a year after winning his fourth-term as CM. A year later, Sukhbir was elevated as deputy CM to his CM father. An astute politician, the senior Badal pushed for Sukhbir's ascent in Akali Dal when he was reigning supreme and was the party's unquestioned leader. For that, he ruthlessly side-lined or co-opted senior party leaders who could have been potential challengers to Sukhbir.'

After ruling the state for fifteen years, from 1997-2002, 2007-2012 and 2012-2017 in alliance with the BJP, the state's oldest party lost the Punjab assembly elections to the youngest party, Aam Admi Party in 2022. Its downslide had started in 2017, but SAD leadership failed to read the warning signals. SAD had lost the assembly polls to the Congress and secured barely eighteen out of 117 seats in alliance with the BJP, two less than the new entrant AAP, a party, born out of activism in neighbouring Delhi.

AAP had displaced the century-old Akali Dal as the main opposition party in the Punjab Legislative Assembly and in 2022, when AAP won the majority, the Congress emerged as the principal opposition in the state and in the 2024 Lok Sabha polls, SAD won just one seat. It had started losing its appeal among the Sikh electorate, particularly the rural peasantry that had traditionally been its core and committed support base.

As the refrain goes, 'victory has many fathers, defeat is an orphan.' Sukhbir learnt his political lessons the hard way. After losing his father, he also lost the public's support and now his legacy is facing a threat.

The election results were announced on 4 June 2024 and guns were out on June 14, within just ten days of the party's rout. A section of leaders, had held frequent meetings and strongly demanded change of leadership, questioning family control of the party. Senior leaders even advised Sukhbir to follow the path of *tyag* (sacrifice) and step down to work to strengthen the party, and reconnect with the disenchanted Sikh community.

Sukhbir refused and retaliated, 'I will never allow power-hungry leaders to succeed in dividing the party of Punjabis and Panth,' while his supporters held counter meetings and passed resolutions hailing his leadership.

Subsequently, some deserted the SAD, some were removed and some new faces were added to the core committee, the highest decision-making body. SAD is not new to rebellion, desertions and divisions in its 104-year-old history.

There is an old saying about Akali Dal—one Akali is a leader, two Akalis are a dal and three Akalis are chaos. Another saying about them is that as and when Akalis are out of power, they quarrel with others and whenever they are in power, they fight with each other.

Despite the ideological fight between the hardliners and the moderates, SAD has remained a force to reckon with in Punjab, irrespective of its electoral losses in recent years. People credit Parkash Singh Badal for keeping the radicals in check, while expanding the secular space for moderates in the party as well as in Panthic politics.

Sukhbir would need his father's acumen, amiability and accessibility to win battles against radicals and rebels to reclaim Panthic support, and unify breakaway factions to emerge as a strong leader of a stronger party. He described the traumatic developments in the party as a conspiracy to weaken SAD and its leadership. He is now back as party president; but can he protect the family legacy?

'Being a party with deep roots in the Punjab countryside, the Akali Dal would survive but the current crisis may be the beginning of the end of the Badal family's dominance in the Panthic party,' observes Ramesh Vinayak.

Vinod Sharma is also of the view that Sukhbir actually lacks the political timber that builds political parties. He is more into money making than earning goodwill of the people. Akali Dal is withering away under his leadership. However, the Akali Dal will stay as parties don't vanish so easily.

AAP may lose its robustness in the next assembly elections because of the quality of their human resources. This would leave space for the BJP, Congress and Akali Dal to grab the spoils.

Before his re-election, Sharma was of the view that Sukhbir would be better off vacating his space in the party for his wife Harsimrat, who is an MP from Bhatinda. She's from the illustrious Majithia clan that itself has a legacy to keep.

Sukhbir won the first challenge retaining control of SAD. The mood at the Maghi Mela on 14 December 2024 had indicated Sukhbir's firmness and the cadre's preference for him to continue leading the party. Now, he faces the bigger challenge of reviving the past glory of the party.

SAD, the oldest regional party of the country, is here to stay with or without the leadership of Sukhbir, who had won his father's legacy but lacks the tact and tenacity to sustain it.

It's not always the case of 'like father like son', or else the pre-Independence era party would not have come to a state where questions would be raised about its future. Akali Dal had many senior leaders to head it, but senior Badal decided on his son who somehow lacked his substance.

Can the dynasty win? A new interesting chapter is starting in the 104-year-old regional party!

Chapter 9

Dalits for Dalits

A Lost Mission

The truncated square Pyramid-shaped building in the prime area of Lucknow, the capital of Uttar Pradesh, has been designed on Buddhist architecture.

It's a temple for Dalits, as portraits of social revolutionaries grace the complex, instead of idols and deities traditionally worshipped in Indian homes and in shrines.

The copper gates, big enough for an elephant to enter, remain shut most of the year, barring big days like Ambedkar Jayanti or Kanshi Ram's anniversary. The crowds are thinning, reflecting the declining health of the BSP, hailed as the country's first political party for Dalits by Dalits.

Mayawati had inaugurated the Bahujan Samaj Kendra, a symbol of Dalit pride and dignity on 3 June 2005, two years before breaking the 14-year-long coalition jinx in the state to form a majority government.

Inscribed on the front wall of the memorial hall is an unconventional will of Kanshi Ram, 'I wish that Km Mayawati should have a long life devoted for the mission she is committed to but as every person has to die one day, she will die too someday.

I wish after her death, her bones would not be immersed in the rivers of Ganga or Yamuna but be laid beside my bones in the Prerna Kendra in Delhi and Lucknow. This wish of mine will go against the Manuvadi system of society and inspire the people of Bahujan Samaj for devotion and respect towards this memorial.'

Mayawati had by then ruled the state thrice and despite her brief tenures, she had socially and politically empowered her core constituency of Dalits enough to cut through the chain of rituals and customs, an offshoot of a discriminatory caste system. No protests were heard from any quarters.

The caste barriers were broken, but the battle started by the social reformer and architect of the Indian Constitution Bhimrao Ramji Ambedkar and continued by her Guru Kanshi Ram was still half won.

Prerna Kendra is just one of the several memorials and parks built in the name of BR Ambedkar and other Dalit icons, including Kanshi Ram with their life-size statues mounted across UP. Mayawati had even unveiled several of her own statues, built and installed on 'public demand.' The sculptures of elephants, her party symbol, dots UP's landscape, which were once covered by the orders of the Election Commission during elections.

When a public interest litigation was filed in the Supreme Court questioning the misuse of public funds on the projects, Mayawati had her list ready of the memorials and monuments built by the Congress government in the name of Nehru-Gandhi, the money spent on the construction of a 182-metre-high statue of Sardar Vallabh Bhai Patel in Gujarat or the proposed statues of Maharana Pratap and Shivaji in Maharashtra.

And while the large-scale architectural memorials and statues were raising countrywide curiosity and controversy because it entailed costs in thousands of crores, Mayawati was asking bureaucrats about the durability of such statues. Will they last 500 years, she had enquired, compelling the construction agencies to replace bricks with red stones. She was perhaps the first CM in the country to use bulldozers for destruction. Overnight, as many as 800 bulldozers were brought from all over the country to clear a sprawling jail complex overnight, as she wanted to build a park in memory of Kanshi Ram.

Now, no government can dare remove these symbols of empowerment. Instead, guards have been deployed for their security.

That was the power of *Dalit ki Beti* who had forcefully silenced her detractors without mincing words, brazenly pursued her Dalit agenda unmindful of the discomfort caused to her partners in governance, chose allies and dumped them at her sweet will, ordered transfer of senior officials from public platforms and made them sing 'happy birthday' when she celebrated her birthdays with aplomb.

Much to the chagrin of her detractors and to the amusement of her supporters, she often rebuked her critics with political rebuttals and ticked them off for not protesting against the use of government funds for celebration of Nehru's birthday as Children's Day or that of Choudhary Charan Singh's as Kisan Day. Could they not tolerate it when the birthday of *Dalit ki Beti* was celebrated as Swabhiman Diwas?

However, the same firebrand Mayawati was tongue-tied when Ambedkar was insulted in December 2024. The BSP leader, who had given voice to docile Dalits in the country, somehow, grew feeble herself.

The Opposition bloc led by Congress and SP were staging countrywide protests demanding the resignation of the Union Home Minister, Amit Shah, for insulting BR Ambedkar, while Mayawati initially addressed a press conference in which the belligerence of yesteryears was missing.

Shedding her inertia, she had later allowed her successor Akash Anand to take to the streets.

Responding to a debate on the Indian Constitution in the Rajya Sabha, the minister had quipped, '*Abhi ek fashion ho gaya hai—Ambedkar, Ambedkar, Ambedkar, Ambedkar—Itna naam bhagwan ka lete to saat janmo tak swarg mil jata.*' (It has become a fashion to say Ambedkar, Ambedkar, Ambedkar, Ambedkar—if they had taken God's name so many times, they would have found a place in heaven).

Earlier, too, Mayawati had committed a political blunder by remaining silent on the raging issue of amendments in the Constitution during the 2024 Lok Sabha elections.

Furious, Dalits had dumped the BSP and supported other non-BJP parties in the elections. The BSP was a big loser.

Has she dropped the mission in quest of power and her personal and family's security?

The 1990s saw Dalit voters of UP uniting under the banner of BSP, which had even emboldened Kanshi Ram to challenge his opponents to divide and rule Bahujan Samaj, saying it was his right to unite them and get their forfeited rights. The same vote bank is today disillusioned and divided.

Kanshi Ram and Mayawati had made huge personal sacrifices to dedicate themselves to the mission of 'Dalit for Dalit'. The founder president of the BSP had taken three vows: Never to marry, never to hold any position and never to buy property.

An officer privy to the information about Kanshi Ram bluntly refusing BJP's offer of the country's Presidentship recalled, 'Sometime in 2002 when Mayawati was CM, Kanshi Ram and I were discussing some official matter at the CM's Kalidas Marg residence when Atal Bihari Vajpayee called Saheb (as Kanshi Ram was addressed) offering him Presidentship of the country. Without batting an eyelid, Kanshi Ram had turned it down, saying, '*Mere mission ka kaam baki hai.*' (My mission is still incomplete.)

The officer said this was not the first time when Kanshi Ram had behaved difficult. He recounted an incident when Mayawati was heading a minority government supported by the BJP from outside in 1995. Much to their embarrassment, CM Mayawati was also pushing her party's Dalit agenda. As long as she was installing statues of their caste heroes, the BJP tolerated it. But the situation turned ugly when Mayawati-Kanshi Ram invoked the name of Ramasamy Periyar, who had led the Dravidian anti-Brahmin movement in Tamil Nadu in the 1960s. The BSP leaders were also firing salvos against Lord Ram and Mahatma Gandhi. The BJP leaders protested, but the BSP high command was unmoved and said they would run the government as they wished.

'Vajpayee called Kanshi Ram a few days before Gandhi Jayanti celebrations at Tilak Hall in the UP Vidhan Bhawan, where he was scheduled to share the dais with Mayawati, who was reluctant to attend the event,' the officer recalled.

In his inimitable style, Vajpayee told Kanshi Ram that any disrespectful comment against Gandhi would compel them to withdraw support to the government.

Kanshi Ram retorted, 'You can withdraw support today, why wait for tomorrow?' Nonetheless, after much counselling by her core team of officers, Mayawati did not make any provocative comment against Gandhi, but concluded her speech stating that as followers of Ambedkar, their beliefs and traditions were different.

The government collapsed on 18 October 1995, after completing 137 days in office, but Kanshi Ram had no regrets as he always said the BSP was not running the government for the benefit of somebody else, but would use every opportunity to reach and rule New Delhi.

Following Kanshi Ram's footsteps, Mayawati had also resolved to dedicate her life to the mission, and sever ties with her family including her parents. She had also taken a pledge not to marry and have her own family as the BSP leader always said, 'The ultimate aim and focus of my life is to see that Bahujan Samaj becomes the rulers and lives a life of dignity. To achieve this, I am ready to sacrifice anything.'

Indeed, she had adopted the Bahujan Samaj as her family.

According to people who worked closely with Mayawati, she maintained distance from her family till early 2000 and they also visited her in Lucknow only once a year on her birthday on January 15. However, as controversies and corruption cases chased her, Mayawati started depending on them, especially her brother Anand Kumar, who never used to appear before the press or public, but was facing the music now.

And in the lust for power, the mission too was lost!

The party survives, but is barely even a regional force. Interestingly, it continues as a national party despite its dismal performance in recent elections. This is how!

After much sweat, the BSP was born

Slow and steady wins the race. This holds true for the BSP, a party that was born on 14 April 1984. It was the brainchild of Kanshi Ram who belonged to Punjab and later worked as a research assistant at the Explosive Research and Development Laboratory in Pune.

Here, he had started a silent revolution for the emancipation of Dalits after he saw caste discrimination at the work place. Initially, he had constituted an SC/ST/OBC/Minorities

Association in the early 1970s. Later, he joined the Republican Party of India for some years, but was soon disillusioned.

Kanshi Ram then formed BAMCEF (All India Backward and Minorities Confederation of Employees Federation) in 1971, officially launched on 6 December 1978 and DS4 (Dalit Shoshit Samaj Sangharsh Samiti) in 1981.

He mobilised government officers and employees across the country who eventually became the party's backbone. Kanshi Ram used to often describe BAMCEF as the brain bank, talent bank and financial bank engaged in the economic and social emancipation of Bahujan Samaj.

Mayawati had joined BAMCEF in 1980 with a dream to fulfil BR Ambedkar's mission of ending caste discrimination and ensuring social justice, when she was in her early 20s. She used to cycle with Kanshi Ram, spreading BSP's message, 'Strength is born from struggle.'

Kanshi Ram's prophecy that she would become a big leader before whom several collectors would line up had actually changed the life of an ambitious Mayawati. She left her home after her father threatened to slam the doors on her if she did not dissociate from Kanshi Ram. 'He can't even make you a Corporator,' he had said angrily.

It was indeed an arduous journey for both Kanshi Ram and Mayawati as they also tested the turbulent waters along with their fledgling BSP. They suffered several personal defeats in elections, but were not disappointed. Every vote polled in their favour gave them the confidence to move forward.

Within eight months of forming the party, the BSP contested the 1984 Lok Sabha elections held in December. The BSP fielded candidates from nine states and three union territories and polled a total of 10.05 lakh votes of which six lakhs came from UP alone.

Kanshi Ram, thereafter, decided to test the waters in Janjgir constituency (then in Madhya Pradesh, now in Chattisgarh), while Mayawati fought from Kairana in UP as an independent candidate. The party was in a nascent stage without a symbol. Kanshi Ram received 9 per cent votes while Mayawati trailed at third position.

They smiled at the bright beginning! While most of the political parties count seats, they counted votes as a marker of their growth.

In 1985, the BSP had contested the Punjab Assembly elections, but their efforts had come to naught. The same year, Mayawati contested the Bijnor Lok Sabha by-election in UP as an independent candidate against Congress heavyweight, Meira Kumar, daughter of the tallest Dalit leader the country has produced, Babu Jagjivan Ram. The other contender was Ram Vilas Paswan from Bihar. Meira Kumar won the seat. Five years later in 1989, Mayawati won from Bijnor constituency, losing the seat to the BJP in 1991, amid the Ram temple frenzy.

Mayawati contested from Hardwar Lok Sabha seat in 1987 and ended up as a runner up. Congress won the seat, Ram Vilas Paswan (Lok Dal) even lost his deposit. By then the BSP was a recognised party with the elephant as its symbol.

Kanshi Ram also contested the 1988 Lok Sabha by-poll from Allahabad constituency against prospective Prime Minister Vishwanath Pratap Singh and Sunil Shastri, son of late Prime Minister Lal Bahadur Shastri. The seat, won in 1984, was vacated by cine star Amitabh Bachchan in the heat of the Bofors scandal. Kanshi Ram polled 69,517 votes in a high profile election won by VP Singh.

Kanshi Ram had also contested the 1989 elections from Amethi Lok Sabha constituency against late Prime Minister Rajiv

Gandhi and Mahatma Gandhi's grandson, Rajmohan Gandhi. He trailed third with 25,400 votes.

Kanshi Ram finally won the 1991 polls from Etawah, the home district of Mulayam Singh Yadav, the founder President of SP. It was here that their friendship had bloomed.

As both the BSP leaders kept losing elections, Kanshi Ram realised the need for funds. At one of his weekly divisional level meetings of the BAMCEF, he spoke about the financial crunch the party was facing against established parties in the elections. He received contributions of Rs 8 crore. The BSP started taking donations which ranged from Rs 1 to Rs 5 as membership fee and after Mayawati came to power, the sky was the limit for donors.

The BSP had opened its account in UP State Assembly elections in 1989, winning thirteen seats and polling 9.41 per cent votes and never looked back again. Even in the heat of the Ayodhya movement in 1991, the BSP had won twelve seats polling 9.44 per cent votes.

In his bid to establish the BSP as the only representative of the Dalits and the downtrodden, Kanshi Ram had extensively travelled the country for months, relentlessly organising caste rallies, small and big, raising provocative slogans and songs that eulogised caste heroes. Dalit writers across the country had also played a humongous role in propagating their mission of bringing the Bahujan Samaj under the banner of BSP.

A silent literary revolution had swept Northern India, helping Dalits mature into a political force to reckon with. As many as 1,500 Dalit writers churned out lakhs of popular booklets, and pamphlets that were savoured by the Dalits, both in the rural and urban areas. In the process, Dalit publishers also mushroomed. The price of the books and booklets ranged between Rs two to Rs fifty. Several editions, each of 5,000 copies, were published to meet their skyrocketing demand. The passionate writers ranged from former governors to bureaucrats, professionals and even small-time masters.

The demolition of the Babri Mosque on 6 December 1992 brought the SP-BSP together and they fought the 1993 elections on a slogan of '*Mile Mulayam Kanshi Ram, Hawa Mein Ud Gaya Jai Sri Ram.*' (When Mulayam and Kanshi Ram come together, the Jai Sri Ram slogan evaporates or vanishes). BJP won 177 seats in a house of 424, but did not get support from other parties to form the government. The SP-BSP coalition with 176 seats formed the government with the support of the Congress and other secular parties.

The BSP with sixty-seven seats was a smaller partner in the coalition government led by Chief Minister Mulayam Singh Yadav. Gradually Mayawati became the de-facto CM, as along with Kanshi Ram, she reviewed the progress of Dalit welfare schemes and publicly chided Mulayam for his lapses.

Mayawati grew ambitious and the coalition had a violent collapse.

The BJP, which had become politically untouchable following the demolition of the disputed shrine in Ayodhya in 1992, extended support to the BSP, paving the way for her midnight swearing in as Chief Minister at Raj Bhavan. The Governor Moti Lal Vora obliged.

Kanshi Ram's struggle had finally fructified when on 3 June 1995, Mayawati became the first Dalit woman CM raising euphoria, not only in the country, but across the globe. Such was her glamour that several UK and US-based organisations vowed to spread her message after her first visit to New York as a member of the Indian delegation for the Inter-Parliamentary Union (IPU) conference.

The government had lasted four months, but the BSP's poll percentage in the subsequent elections in 1996 rose to 19.64 per cent, without increasing the seat tally of sixty-seven that they had won in 1993.

Intriguingly, the BSP had allied with the Congress, but the two together had failed to get the requisite majority to form the government in the 1996 polls. While the state was under President's Rule, Kanshi Ram and Mayawati quietly struck a deal with the same communal forces, the BJP, they had pledged to eliminate from the state's politics.

The BSP leadership had then produced an innovative plan of ruling the state on a six-monthly rotation basis. Mayawati governed the state for the first six months during which she had zealously pushed her Dalit agenda, while BJP's Kalyan Singh, the one-time national hero of the saffron brigade, sulked at home. Mayawati reluctantly handed over the baton, adhering to the advice of some bureaucrats.

The contentious issue between the partners was the strict implementation of the SC/ST Act by Mayawati in which upper caste people were penalised/jailed even on flimsy complaints ranging from slapping, beating, or humiliation of Dalits.

Kalyan Singh revoked the act within twenty-four hours and she withdrew support within twenty-eight days.

Singh who had taken charge of the CM's office on 21 September 1997, revoked the ordinance on September 23 while Mayawati withdrew support on 21 October 1997.

Kalyan Singh retaliated, broke parties and secured a majority. He even divided the BSP, though she had kept her party MLAs at the CM's bungalow, the safest haven.

Interestingly, Mayawati later revealed the reason behind their two pre-electoral alliances in 22 years of BSP's existence.

She said the first alliance was sewed with Mulayam Singh Yadav with a dual purpose—first, to unite the Bahujan Samaj under the leadership of someone from their Samaj (Mulayam was a backward) and second to checkmate the BJP's rise on the temple issue. However, the experiment failed because of Mulayam's selfish politics. What she did not say was that the BJP had also fanned her huge hunger for power. The second alliance was done with the Congress after the country's Prime Minister and Congress President, PV Narasimha Rao, went knocking at Kanshi Ram's doors.

In the 2002 polls, the BSP won ninety-eight seats and polled 23.19 per cent votes. Mayawati once again allied with the BJP and formed the government that lasted one year and 118 days. This time, she had refused to succumb to BJP's pressure for tying BSP into a national alliance for the 2004 Lok Sabha elections.

In her brand of politics, it was not the numbers in the Vidhan Sabha that propelled the BSP to power thrice, but sheer backroom manoeuvrings or political blackmailing.

Both the BSP leaders had suffered untouchability all their lives, but they had no untouchables in the political domain.

Kanshi Ram used Uttar Pradesh as a laboratory in which he did political experiments and churned out formulas to grab power. He often said, 'We want *mazboor sarkars (lame governments) and not mazboot sarkars* (strong governments) till the time the Bahujan Samaj is in a position to form its own government.'

His slogan was, '*vote se lenge PM/CM, arakshan se lenge SP/ DM* (We will get PM/CM positions through votes and DM/SP posts by quota).

Kanshi Ram died on 9 October 2006 after a prolonged sickness. After a brief battle over his legacy with his family, Mayawati became the undisputed leader of the BSP. The family formed Sahib Shri Kanshi Ramji Bachchao Sangharsh Samiti and had even petitioned the President and the Prime Minister accusing Mayawati of forcibly keeping an ailing Kanshi Ram at her house. While inviting me to her home in a rare gesture, she had said she was taking care of her Guru better than what a son would have done.

However, the legacy episode did not last long as the BSP founder president had not left any ambiguity about his successor. He had handed over the torch to Mayawati on 15 January 2001 at a public function in Lucknow.

Kanshi Ram chose her as she was a Jatav, a dominant caste in UP and because of her commitment to the mission. Sometimes, he used to fear disintegration of the party after his death.

His fears are partly coming true as the party has not disintegrated, but weakened.

While holding the urn with his ashes on 19 October 2006, Mayawati had declared, 'I lit his pyre and affirm I would complete his mission. He wanted to see a BSP government in the state and at the Centre by uniting people who wanted an egalitarian society.'

The urn with his ashes were kept at the Bahujan Samaj Prerna Kendra!

Mayawati had partially fulfilled his dream by forming a majority BSP government in 2007, but gradually deviated from his path as she craved for power for herself and not for the Bahujan Samaj.

The BSP won 206 seats of the 403 seats in the UP Assembly in 2007, polling 30.43 per cent votes.

She could never taste power again as she had compromised with the principles and the philosophy of the party. The BSP remained in demand as political parties wanted Dalit votes, not to make a CM or PM.

The BSP, which had once raised the slogan of *Tilak Taraju aur Talwar, Inko Maro Jute Char*, (loosely translated, it means: Shun or hit Brahmins, Banias and Thakurs with shoes) opened its doors for Brahmins to build a winning coalition of Dalits, Brahmins and Muslims. The Brahmin face of the party was SC Mishra, who had toured over 20,000 kms in the state, organising Dalit-Brahmin *bhoj*, while Naseemuddin Siddiqui held closed door meetings with the Muslims to solicit their support. The social engineering paved the way for the formation of a majority government of the BSP for the first time in 2007, without any borrowed crutches.

The BSP grew ambitious after the 2007 victory as people saw Mayawati's potential to grow as a national leader, next to Jagjivan Ram. Her victory had activated BSP units in Rajasthan and Madhya Pradesh as well.

Kanshi Ram had already established the party's foundation in the two states, which had a committed cadre who had cycled with him hundreds of kilometres to build the support base.

Kanshi Ram had frequently visited Bhopal, Jabalpur and Sagar in the mid-1970s with boxes of pamphlets to mobilise workers for BAMCEF. Their slogans were provocative, reflecting their anger against the caste system. These faceless workers were tailors and technicians, lawyers and teachers, shop keepers, car mechanics, *et al.*

Many believed the BAMCEF had withered away after multiple splits since the BSP came into existence. But the original BAMCEF, despite the splits, remained the backbone of Mayawati's political movement. It silently worked as a 'shadow' organisation in several states.

To safeguard activists (majority government servants) from disciplinary action by unfriendly governments, the state units had listed their spouses as members. Mayawati had handsomely rewarded them during ticket distribution in the 2008 Rajasthan Assembly polls. Over two dozen candidates were either government employees themselves, who had retired or resigned to contest elections, or their kin.

However, the bi-polar states failed to accept the BSP and few who were elected easily defected to the ruling party. Maharashtra too had rejected the BSP as it was the land of Ambedkar and the state had their own Dalit leadership.

Mayawati also failed to nurture the support base built by Kanshi Ram in several states, as she got bogged down with the construction of memorials and parks in UP.

She, thus, lost a golden opportunity to emerge as the most powerful and popular Dalit leader at the national level. Unlike Kanshi Ram, Mayawati had short-term vision for short-term gains. She, however, protected her party from being subsumed by rivals.

The BSP had drawn its strength from a committed cadre, a strong party network and a dependable set of Dalit officers. She knew the Bahujan Samaj had risen as a political force.

'Just as the BSP today is a symbol of Bahujan Samaj's dignity, Mayawati, in the opinion of intellectuals, has acquired such a standing in Indian politics wherein people may criticise her, even condemn her, but nobody can ignore her,' Mayawati wrote in her popular book, *Mere Sangharshmay Jeevan Evam Bahujan Movement ka Safarnaama*.

The elephantine fall

The BSP's downslide had started from the 2012 UP Assembly elections when the poll percentage dropped to 26 per cent from 30.5 per cent in 2007 and from 206 seats to barely eighty in a house of 403. In the subsequent state elections in 2017 and 2022, the BSP showed no signs of recovery. Mayawati experimented with alliances, but failed.

In the 2017 Assembly elections, Mayawati went solo against the BJP and Congress-SP combine. The party's vote percentage was down by about 3 per cent, as the BSP polled 20.33 per cent votes and won nineteen seats.

In 2022, the BSP could barely win one seat polling 12.88 per cent votes.

Coming to the 2014 General Elections, the BSP had polled 19.77 per cent votes with no seat in the kitty.

Alarmed by her party's continuous downslide as well as under pressure from the Muslim community, Mayawati entered into an alliance with her bete noire Mulayam Singh Yadav and formed a formidable SP-BSP-RLD coalition to take on the BJP in the 2019 Lok Sabha elections. But what looked like a cakewalk on paper became a damp squib in the poll arena. A simple arithmetic had put the coalition in an advantageous position, as their combined votes of the 2014 Lok Sabha polls had added to 42.98 per cent, a little higher than 42.63 per cent of the BJP.

The leaders exchanged flowers and sent apt messages to their cadres. But mistrust still prevailed. Mayawati could not or did not transfer her votes to SP nominees. Thus, while the BSP could win ten seats polling 19.43 per cent votes, the SP had to contend with five seats polling 18.11 per cent votes. The alliance snapped.

In the 2024 General Elections, the BSP's decision to go alone had upset her voters as other opposition parties had formed I.N.D.I.A (Indian National Developmental Inclusive Alliance) at the national level to defeat the BJP-led National Democratic Alliance and its divisive politics. The BSP couldn't win a single seat and the vote percentage also fell down to 9.35 per cent.

There were logical reasons. Dalits had never demanded Mayawati to visit sites of atrocities or Dalit victims of rapes and riots, but in 2024, they had desperately demanded her intervention to stop the BJP on its tracks as they were fearing amendments in Ambedkar's Constitution and end of quotas after they procured 400-plus seats.

Mayawati had not only disappointed them with her lacklustre campaigning, but she had also failed to respond to their appeals. As their *behenji* frequently changed party candidates, purportedly to harm the Cong-SP alliance, and withdrew her nephew Akash Anand from campaigning after his fiery speech against the PM and the UP CM inviting BJP's wrath, her voters suspected a tacit understanding of their own party with the BJP Party that they wanted to defeat.

Why, they asked? Was it to save her brother Anand Kumar from incarceration in corruption cases lodged against him? What about the mission, the Constitution that had given them fundamental rights?

Mayawati's core voters—the Jatavs—who had continued to stand behind her like a rock, divided, as BSP had literally gone missing from the battlefield. Some voted for the opposition bloc to protect the Constitution, others for the BJP's welfare schemes.

Still, they did not completely dump the BSP, which managed to get 9.35 per cent votes in an election in which other castes deserted her and rejected her winning formula of core votes plus the candidate's votes.

Despite its dismal performances in the elections, the BSP remained in demand as Mayawati is the only leader in the country, who by one message to her supporters can transfer her valuable votes to her poll partner.

One of the founder-members of the BSP, RK Chaudhary,

who had closely worked with Kanshi Ram and Mayawati, told the media after the 2024 polls, 'The core Dalit politics has become leaderless in the state and in the coming days, the SP would carry forward the flame of Bahujanism awakened by Kanshi Ram.' He is now an SP MP. In another interview to the PTI, he had said:

> Mayawati has been our leader. We respect her. But if anyone has ended Kanshi Ramji's movement, it is behenji. When Kanshi Ram was alive, while he was capable of running Babasaheb Ambedkar's mission, the Bahujan Samaj was not mentally prepared or ready for it. Now, when the Samaj knows about the Constitution, reservation and their rights, there was no one to lead them. As far as the core leadership position is concerned, I think the space is vacant and whoever makes efforts would lead them. (*PTI*, 16 June 2024)

A wakeup call for Mayawati

The organisational structure built by Kanshi Ram from the central to the booth level had a clearly laid out hierarchy and style of functioning. It was led by party coordinators from state to zonal, divisional, district, tehsil, block, village and booth level, whose voice had mattered more in the party affairs than those of the ministers. Even Mayawati used to hold regular meetings of the coordinators till 2003. Thereafter, these meetings became irregular, as she started relying heavily on BSP National General Secretary Satish Chandra Mishra, who also handled the court cases.

Few, perhaps, may know that even Mayawati used to keep the mobile numbers of all her party coordinators in the country. 'Three registers are maintained—one each at the national and state party offices and one with Mayawati. She calls office-bearers even at odd hours for first-hand information about the party's mission,' an office bearer had told me in Rajasthan.

She also ensured the coordinators had motor-cycles and cell phones for better connectivity. An office bearer said, 'Behenji's messages go faster than a telegram—it travels within minutes across the country.'

Will she be able to recover as waiting in the wings are several claimants of her vote bank? While the BJP hopes to create a permanent Dalit vote bank through their beneficiary schemes, the Samajwadi Party's PDA (*Pichra Dalit and Alpasankhyak*) strategy also had great traction in 2024.

Kanshi Ram used to say the Bahujan comprises of 6,000 castes and constitutes 85 per cent of the population.

Another claimant of Kanshi Ram's legacy, Chandrashekhar Azad, after his maiden victory from Nagina Lok Sabha constituency in 2024, would roar in Parliament on SC/ST issues, while the BSP would be missing in action. Dalits have always wanted their leaders to be firebrands, a quality that used to attract them towards Mayawati.

Thirty-one-year-old Chandrashekhar Azad, the founder of the Azad Samaj Party, has been pursuing Dalit politics since the formation of his party four years ago. But it lacks the organisational network of BSP and BAMCEF, which is active again to save it from sinking. An effort is on to reunite the splinter groups.

In the 2027 Assembly polls, the BSP can still become the first choice of Dalits if Mayawati succeeds in shedding its BJP's B-party tag, as they realise the fact that the BSP was the only party by Dalits for Dalits in the country.

JNU professor Vivek Kumar had summed up the reasons behind this rising phenomenon in his book, *India's Roaring Revolution: Dalit Assertion and New Horizons.* He writes:

> The BSP represents the new horizon of Dalit assertion, that Dalits can also come to power and in fact rule by forming their own political party, they can also represent themselves independently, which is qualitatively different from being in a party led and dominated by the so-called upper strata and then represented by them for their socio-political rights. It is true before the advent of BSP, Dalits never thought of contesting elections independently even for panchayats. They were given patronage either by the landlord, or the dominant castes or political parties, dominated by upper castes. But now Dalits not only contest elections from panchayat to Parliament on their own, but they are also nursing the aspiration of becoming ministers, chief ministers and even prime minister through a political party led and dominated by the Dalits. BSP became the first national political party established by Dalits.

Would Mayawati lose propriety rights on Dalits that she has enjoyed since the 1980s and in the process, wind up a unique party?

Earlier, political expert Prof Badri Narayan Tiwari, who has written a book on Kanshi Ram had said, 'Despite desertions hitting the party from time to time, the BSP has always grown in strength. Don't write her off as BSP is a party driven by the cadre and not the leaders.'

True, she has cadres and committed voters for whom election is a war. They have been indoctrinated by the BSP leadership not to rest or eat till they have won the battle by getting all votes cast on the polling day. Her voters are willing to give BSP one more chance, as they see some hope in her nephew, Akash Anand, whom she had announced as her successor and removed later. But she has to trust him as Kanshi Ram had trusted her.

One of the founder members of the BSP, Rishikar Bharti lives in Korba in Chattisgarh. He knew Kanshi Ram since 1984, when he had contested from the Janjgir Lok Sabha constituency. He had told *ETV Bharat*, Chattisgarh on 9 April 2024:

> After Kanshi Ram's death, the BSP had split into several parts with most of the founder members forming their own parties. Today, there are about 150 parties registered in the name of Bahujan Samaj. We are trying to unite them. I claim with conviction that even today if Mayawati shows determination and we are able to unite all the founder-members or their successors, then we can make Mayawati Prime Minister of the country. We are the majority class. This party can be revived anytime, we don't need any preparations.

Rishikar Bharti has reminded Mayawati of their dream, 'We are trying hard to give India its first Dalit Prime Minister in the next twelve-thirteen years, a man or a woman.' But she will have to shed her fears and return to the streets in her original firebrand style. No government would dare send her to jail and if they did, she will emerge as a force to reckon with at the national level. Also, to improve her political credibility, either she will have to bargain and join the BJP's bandwagon or dump and denounce it. Time is ripe for her to make the right choice.

As with this, is linked the Dalit mission.

To sum up, regional parties don't die, but they fade away if they fail to read the writing on the wall.

Chapter 10

AAP
Flying with Clipped Wings

The Aam Aadmi Party originated from a public movement against corruption without any defined ideology or identity of a region, religion or caste.

Born in the afterglow of the common man's fight against corruption, the unique party was aptly named the Aam Aadmi Party. It was instantly lapped up by India's working class as its style of functioning was starkly different from traditional parties.

Ironically, after achieving incredible electoral success, including the enviable status of a 'national party' within just 10 years of contesting its first election, AAP had to battle charges for the very vice it had stood up to fight. The most disconcerting charge Kejriwal had to face in the run up to the do-or-die 2025 Delhi Assembly elections was of corruption in a liquor policy scam. His public image was tarnished as for someone who had always advocated austerity in public life was also accused of splurging money on converting his official residence into a *sheesh mahal* (a palace of glass). Kejriwal and his party responded with the Raj Mahal jibe in which they accused the Prime Minister of living in a Rs 2,700-crore lavish house. The public was not amused as their expectations from Kejriwal were high as he was one of them. And the corruption charges against the AAP ministers haunted them.

Senior leaders of the party were sent to jail, including founder convenor Arvind Kejriwal, himself, who received temporary reprieve from the courts at the last minute. But damage had been done to their impeccable reputation. Sometimes, people start believing oft-repeated accusations, whether true or false, as Goebbels' truth.

AAP was often described as the country's first political unicorn or start-up, which made huge profits from its one-off investments in planning and strategies, but ahead of the 2025 Delhi polls, it had come on the verge of bankruptcy, from which only investors could bail them out.

The leadership faced a huge credibility crisis. Arvind Kejriwal went to the public court with a vengeance for a clean chit and to repair their public image. 'Why would we go for crowdfunding if we were corrupt,' has been AAP's consistent response to corruption allegations against the senior leadership. It was crucial for him and his party to clear the corruption charge.

Moreover, the 2025 Delhi Assembly elections were also crucial for restoration of public faith in alternative politics that the Common Man's Party (AAP) represented. Any failure in this election, would bring in a dark phase for Arvind Kejriwal, the fulcrum of the anti-corruption movement, as well as cast a shadow on the future of AAP. Before the results were known, political expert Mukesh Kumar had forecasted that APP will not divide, but without Kejriwal, the party may not even survive.

It was a triangular contest with the BJP and the Congress. While the BJP looked determined to win Delhi, the Congress had put up a half-hearted fight, more to defeat Kejriwal than stop the BJP from coming to power. However, if AAP made a comeback despite the odds in the fray, it would not have been a loss of just another election, but a definite loss of face for both the contenders.

The general perception before the announcement of the Delhi polls was that AAP would return to power, riding a sympathy wave in favour of Kejriwal. By the time voters went to the polling booth, it had largely subsided. AAP also faced a 10-year-long anti-incumbency factor, along with the corruption charges. Their spirits were high, and prospects, dim.

The results did not come as a shocker. The BJP won forty-eight seats while the remainder twenty-two went to AAP. The Congress failed to open its account.

The determined voters of Delhi delivered a decisive mandate, which left no ambiguity about their anger and unhappiness with the party they had supported to the hilt in the past and felt miserably betrayed. They refused to give a clean chit to Arvind Kejriwal and defeated him and his close lieutenant Manish Sisodia. While redefining the political and power structure of the country's capital, they rewarded BJP with an opportunity to serve.

In his 2018 book, *Republic of Caste*, Anand Teltumbde described the Aam Aadmi Party as 'A political App for the Neoliberal era.' It was a telling analogy. Like a mobile application, the AAP's political package seemed to offer a range of functionalities to its citizen consumers, which centred on improving quality of public goods, like health and education, along with subsidised provision of welfare services like electricity, drinking water and transportation. In the book, Teltumbde wrote, 'The biggest challenge before a fledgling entity is to scale up or be gobbled by the biggest shark. Remember what Microsoft did to Netscape or what Amazon is doing to Flipkart.'

BJP had been striving hard to capture Delhi and they did. Yogendra Yadav, who had fallen out of favour with the party leadership told the media that though Kejriwal had no ethical bone in his body, he did have a serious capacity to fight back and rebuild the party. This comes as a consolation to the party volunteers, but is Kejriwal willing to listen?

When the common man embraced activism

At the time of its inception in 2012, AAP had represented urban India and was founded by the common man with no political lineage, leanings or trappings of power. People easily identified with its leadership as it emerged from the crowds—students, professionals, lawyers, journalists and former bureaucrats. The widespread corruption they faced in every sphere of life had turned them into activists, thronging the streets of Delhi with the tricolour in their hands during the 2011 anti-corruption protests.

India was rising against corruption

The India Against Corruption movement was a rare occasion in Indian history that brought people from across the spectrum on the same platform. The protests that established base in the heart of Delhi, at the Ramlila Maidan, saw participation of the rich and poor, activists and bankers, students and home makers. People came out of curiosity, while others felt the burning desire to shatter the shackles of red-tapism and corruption in both the administrative and political systems. As the fever caught on, some took long leave from their jobs, while others quit them entirely to join the movement, clueless about where it would end or what it could achieve, but happy in the knowledge that they were becoming part of a milestone in post-Independence India.

These were people who wanted to be the harbingers of

change, harbouring no cravings for personal aggrandisement. The movement itself was funded by the people.

The man on the street thus had high hopes from AAP, India Against Corrpution's breakaway faction that chose to join mainstream politics, as they wore a different cap. They neither talked loud nor big. Instead, their public discourses revolved around the need to change the corrupt system that deprived the common man of his rightful dues—power, water, health services and good education. Their slogan was, *Mujhe Swarajya Chahiye* and *Mein Aam Aadmi Hun*. (I want self-rule, self governance and I am the common man.)

The top line on AAP's website, *AAP Ka Ram Rajya*, succinctly revealed their politics and promises. Born amid BJP's chants of *Jai Sri Ram*, it was also its subtle response.

The face of the anti-corruption movement was Anna Hazare whose multiple protests and hunger strikes in Delhi since April 2011 had taken the country by storm, but the brain behind it was that of Arvind Kejriwal. Other important leaders of his team were Prashant Bhushan, Ramdev, Kumar Vishwas, Yogendra Yadav and tens of thousands of invisible ones.

To many, Anna resembled Gandhi, the Father of the Nation, who was out on a similar mission. Gandhi had fought for the country's freedom while Anna, a Gandhian himself, was crusading for freedom from corruption. He was demanding the government to pass tougher laws to check corruption.

On 15 August 2011, hours before he was to embark on an indefinite fast to demand strong anti-corruption laws, Anna Hazare was detained by the Delhi Police, triggering large-scale protests across the country.

However, a resilient Anna refused to leave jail till the government introduced stronger laws to check corruption. He walked out of the jail on 19 August 2011, only after the government moved a resolution in Parliament, accepting his three demands that included a Citizen's Charter and establishment of Lokayuktas in states. A public debate on the Lokpal Bill was also organised.

By December 2011, a decision was taken by the team to shift the protest from Delhi to Mumbai, as it had become too cold. The show flopped.

Senior income tax official Arvind Kejriwal and ex-cop Kiran Bedi remained Anna's close lieutenants, but differences started cropping up over the contentious issue of entering mainstream politics.

Anna Hazare was against the move from the very beginning. In fact, he often displayed his aversion to politicians by not letting them share the dais.

The BJP, which was in the opposition, gave tacit support to the movement but was soon accused of exploiting the Anna Hazare team to overthrow the Congress government, then in the middle of its second term under Prime Minister Manmohan Singh. It was already in a mess with scams tumbling out of its cupboards.

As the Congress government stubbornly refused to relent on their demands, Kejriwal said the only way to change the system was to become a part of it, by plunging into politics and forming a government. When Anna Hazare had started the anti-corruption movement, Congress had often taunted them saying, 'protesting on streets, raising slogans was easier than contesting elections and facing Parliament.'

The AAP website notes, 'Arvind Kejriwal decided that the only way to rid this country of corruption was to join politics, enter government, and clean up the system from within. Thus, on 2 October 2012, the journey of the anti-corruption protest towards the political revolution called the Aam Aadmi Party began.' A faction was against the move.

A senior AAP functionary said initially even Anna Hazare was on the same page with Kejriwal on entering politics, but soon shifted his stand. Hazare was present on the dais from where Arvind Kejriwal had announced their street to parliament movement to purify the Lok Sabha. He endorsed the decision, only after which the 16-month-old India Against Corruption movement was called off.

Amidst loud cheering from the crowds at Jantar Mantar on 31 July 2012, Anna Hazare had clearly said though he would not launch a party or contest elections, he would travel across the country to build an alternative party.

In September 2012, Anna had walked out of the meeting convened at the Constitution Club, while warning Kejriwal and team to not use his photos anywhere. The spearheads of the anti-corruption mission split into two teams—Team Anna, who was against taking a plunge into politics and Team Kejriwal, who believed their fight would remain incomplete till they took the bull by the horns after entering politics. As such, it was not a very cohesive team and was plagued with ideological differences. Some had distinct left leanings.

Amid dissenting voices, the formation of a political party was announced on 2 October 2012 and was formally launched on 26 November 2012. Delhi Assembly elections were due in less than a year's time.

In a grandstanding that later became a cornerstone of his politics, Kejriwal said, 'We will not build our manifestoes sitting in air-conditioned cabins but will go around the country and take public opinion.'

Emphasising on their principle of participatory politics, Kejriwal had also said the public would decide the candidates and also fund the elections.

Before and after the formation of the political party, many of his associates, who had tirelessly worked for the cause, deserted him but the public welcomed the 'refreshing change' in the politics of the country and supported the 'Common Man's Party,' as it promised cheaper electricity, free water and better education and health facilities.

Within one year of its formation, AAP fought its first Delhi Assembly Elections in 2013.

Kejriwal's team had novel ideas to contest the election. They mapped the entire New Delhi constituency from where he had challenged Sheila Dikshit and were ready with the basics of the constituents much before the elections were announced—the profiles of voters, their addresses, their leanings, their cell members, their interests and so on.

A member of the team said that AAP's micro-macro planning was so penetrating that Dikshit's sister and her campaign manager, within three days of campaigning in the constituency, had privately conceded defeat. In an internal party meeting, she confessed, 'It's a lost election.'

The Congress, in its overconfidence, made a blunder by underestimating Kejriwal. While some big names and faces used to make grand appearances at both the anti-corruption protest site and also for the campaigning, the actual ground work for the party's maiden elections was done completely by Kejriwal and his team of young and old volunteers.

How the common man contributed

A supporter had offered his two-storied building behind Hanuman Mandir in central Delhi to AAP to run its office at no cost. The iconic building, now no longer with AAP, broke all stereotypes of a political party office. In addition to white shirt, trouser and canvas shoes, politicians quitting their parent parties in the hope of easy tickets, the building had also become a melting ground of people from all walks of life who saw in AAP the possibility of an *aam aadmi* entering the political arena.

It was a proverbial *shadi ka ghar*, where skit and flash mob practices took place in one room, while the adjacent room would be hosting a meeting between senior leaders. There was a perpetual shortage of chairs and cushions for waiting people, and those taking time off, slept too.

A journalist who had covered the electrifying elections recalled how the building used to hum with activity round the clock with volunteers excitedly assembling, chatting and sharing information, taking quick meals at a running *langar*, before picking up the publicity material and darting off for campaigning again. In Gandhian style, everyone was invited to eat and everyone who ate would stand in a line to wash their utensils. The place was always filled with fun and laughter, even as the core team occupied various corners and brainstormed.

Perhaps, the BJP had also not taken AAP and its leader Kejriwal seriously, as they even failed to fathom the determination of the volunteers, who had earlier joined his crusade against corruption.

Most of the volunteers were young as well as apolitical and thus their campaign style was also different from routine speeches, and big rallies of established political parties. AAP brought back the culture of *nukkad sabhas* (street corner meetings) and door-to-door campaigning. The young sang their hearts out in support of AAP, played guitars, organised flash mobs and used social media extensively and innovatively to popularise AAP's promises that ranged from sops to services. The party symbol, the broom, found at every home, resonated with everyone.

AAP had a headstart over its rivals, as it decided most of its candidates much in advance and its campaign was volunteer-based. The messaging, both online and offline, had started when the rivals were deciding their candidates and campaign plans. Everything was simple.

A Narendra Modi wave was beginning to grip Delhi, but both the Congress and the BJP lacked fresh faces at the state level to invigorate their campaigns.

AAP won twenty-eight of the seventy seats. The muffler man, Arvind Kejriwal, emerged as a giant killer, defeating widely popular three-time Congress Chief Minister Sheila Dikshit. Many had prophesised, 'He would be finished even before the take off.' Dikshit herself had asked, 'Who is Arvind Kejriwal?'—only to be defeated by him when results were announced on 8 December 2013.

A party with a difference was born. Politics was no longer an exclusive domain of *netas*.

However, here seasoned politics turned the tables on the political novice. Even though the BJP had emerged as the single largest party winning most seats, it did not stake claim to form the government as it had lacked a clear majority. Congress, even though it had been humiliated by AAP, offered 'outside' support to the fledgling party, pushing AAP to run the sensitive capital, hoping that it would fail.

But prior to accepting the Congress offer to form the government, AAP launched yet another public campaign called 'Should we form the government,' as they had so far pursued participatory politics.

After a big yes from the people who thronged their big and small rallies, AAP formed the government and Kejriwal was sworn in as Chief Minister in December 2013.

The government collapsed in forty-nine days after Congress refused to support its Jan Lokpal Bill in the Assembly. AAP also learned the hard way that the middle class, which supported its anti-corruption movement, was largely status quoist and did not take too kindly to the sops like free water and power schemes that it had announced or its new style of governance. The poor and the slums benefitted and eventually they became core voters of AAP.

The one thing that did stand out, however, was a marked reduction in corruption in the first few days.

President's Rule was imposed in Delhi on14 February 2014 and lasted for full one year. In the 2015 Assembly polls, AAP returned with an unexpected landslide victory, winning sixty-seven out of seventy seats. The Jan Lokpal Bill was moved and passed by the Delhi Assembly on 4 December 2015.

In between, AAP was hit by internecine troubles. The founder members, Yogendra Yadav, and Prashant Bhushan along with Anand Kumar and Ajit Jha were expelled from the party for indulging in anti-party activities. They were first given a show cause notice and later expelled after their explanations were not found tenable. One of the charges against them was conspiring to remove Arvind Kejriwal, who had by then become Delhi CM, from the party convenor's position. Senior advocate Prashant Bhushan had expressed his fears about the common man's party turning into a one-man party, as Kejriwal was growing increasingly inaccessible and dictatorial in political decisions and policy making.

Undoubtedly, after the spectacular victory in the Delhi elections, Kejriwal had grown ambitious, as the 'giant killer' wanted to make another kill in Varanasi in the 2014 Lok Sabha elections. He decided to take on the BJP's prime ministerial candidate Narendra Modi. The party contested 400 seats including Varanasi, which they lost. AAP won four seats in Punjab, the state which they could embrace with some effort.

AAP contested Goa and Punjab Assembly polls in 2017. It did not win any seat in Goa, but won twenty seats in Punjab, which further emboldened Kejriwal to continue his focus on the state. The party also contested forty seats in several states in the 2019 General Polls, but could win only in one.

Alongside, the young ministers in Delhi went into an overdrive, launching several people-centric schemes. In the 2020 assembly elections, AAP came back with sixty-two out of seventy seats.

Senior journalist Pankaj Vohra, who closely follows Delhi and its politics, said the national parties were obviously flustered as AAP became the first party in the country to acquire more than 50 per cent of the votes polled in two successive assembly elections. Political parties rarely manage to secure such overwhelming support, reflected in the votes polled in their favour.

AAP, driven by a restless Arvind Kejriwal, was in a hurry to spread its tentacles in the country. It looked at Gujarat, Prime Minister Narendra Modi's home state as well as the prosperous Punjab. Kejriwal loved challenges—the bigger the challenge, the happier he was.

Kejriwal, who had high diabetes and a perpetual cough, decided to go for medical treatment—detoxification therapy for his chronic cough, diabetes and asthma at a naturopathy centre in Bengaluru for about ten days and came back, rejuvenated.

After the cure, Kejriwal, the man on a mission, was unstoppable. He was slapped in public, a shoe and ink was thrown on him, but he kept chasing his dream, howsoever, unpragmatic.

Kejriwal displayed his anathema to ostentation, and travelled in his small blue WagonR. However, though he claimed he wanted to shun VIP culture, he somehow failed as the paraphernalia that accompanied him as CM increased by the day. And then 'Sheesh Mahal' was built. Before the 2025 Assembly polls, BJP used the Comptroller and Auditor General report to embarrass Kejriwal by raising 139 questions on the Rs 33.86 crore spent on the renovation of his official bungalow. AAP leaders hit back describing Prime Minister's bungalow as Raj Mahal, but somehow the allegations and counter allegations had instead further hurt his already 'battered' image by his incarceration in the liquor scam. He is out on bail; some believed the charges, while some did not.

Kejriwal should have shunned nepotism plaguing the one-man regional parties in the country, but he also preferred his bureaucrat wife Sunita Kejriwal to unofficially hold charge of the CM's office while he was in jail.

While praising his wife's devotion and discipline in handling the party as well as family affairs in his absence, Kejriwal had said that Sunita had kept the motivation of the cadre high and remained an important link between him and the party leaders. However, by appointing Atishi as CM after his release from jail, he tried to nullify the accusations.

Political expert Mukesh Kumar had said that 'the Kejriwal couple is holding and controlling the party. His wife is having discussions with opposition leaders, sharing the dais with them. The message is clear and there is no opposition.'

Many who did not understand the why, which Kejriwal later described, also saw her elevation in the same perspective.

Sunita, herself, an IRS officer had silently played the game to perfection, gaining sympathy of the people while managing the show in his absence.

She never ever looked as if she was hungry for power. Perhaps, everyone knew that she was a stop-gap arrangement.

Fighting the taint

Since 2013, APP without any visible organisational structure, had remained on a progression path till 2023, when its leaders were put behind bars in the Delhi Excise scam.

Within a record time of 10 years since its inception, the Election Commission of India, after much delay, had recognised AAP as a national party on 10 April 2023, albeit after the High Court's directions. A 10-year-old party is considered young, if not in its infancy in the Indian context.

Kejrwal had then described their electoral feat as a 'miracle.' Many regional parties aspire to acquire the national party status and fail. The Shiromani Akali Dal of Punjab is the oldest regional party born much before the country's Independence, but remains a state party. It's on the decline now as AAP rules Punjab.

AAP is also a state party in Gujarat, Punjab, Delhi and Goa. While AAP has formed state governments in Punjab besides Delhi, in Gujarat, which is the Prime Minister's home state, the party had polled 12.92 per cent votes and won five seats in the 2022 Gujarat Assembly polls. It polled 6.77 per cent votes in Goa and had picked up two seats in the same year.

Ironically, the anti-corruption crusader and a populist CM is now accused of corruption and is out on bail. The Enforcement Directorate in its statement in the court, described him as the 'Kingpin and Key Conspirator of the Delhi Excise Scam.' The Central Bureau of Investigation had also submitted its report in the case. Two of his key strategists—the former deputy Chief Minister Manish Sisodia and Health Minister Satyendra Jain also remained endlessly in jail.

The expelled leaders, Prashant Bhushan and Yogendra Yadav had condemned Kejriwal's arrest, describing it as a 'murder of democracy,' but Anna Hazare was not so kind. He had said that the arrest was expected.

The Supreme Court released Sisodia on 9 August 2024 after he had spent seventeen months in jail. Another key leader, Sanjay Singh, a Rajya Sabha member from Delhi, was also sent to jail in October 2023 in the money laundering case connected with the Delhi excise scam, but was released in April 2024. After his release, a few weeks before the general elections, Sanjay Singh gave a forceful speech aimed at energising the dormant party and demoralised workers.

Sisodia was back in action, cultivating the ground for their contest in the Delhi polls in 2025. His release instantly changed the mood and the morale of the cadres and despite heavy rains on 9 August 2024, the public and the cadre celebrated his freedom.

Sisodia in his inspiring speech said, 'I have been saying since my freedom from jail that we are all horses of the chariot. Our real charioteer is in jail right now. They locked us in jail, but they could never lock us out of the heart of the people.'

Sanjay Singh, while mocking those who dismissed Sisodia's release from jail as just bail, took promises from one and all to meet and greet every BJP leader after winning the Delhi polls with, '*bas zamanat hi to zapt hui hai*' (only deposit has been forfeited). He raised the slogan with which AAP had grown, '*bhrashtachar ka ek hi kaal, Kejriwal, Kejriwal*.' (Only Kejriwal can end corruption.)

After much confusion about Kejriwal's resignation after his incarceration, the party leader and minister Atishi said 'Arvind Kejriwal was Delhi CM, is CM and will always be Delhi CM. He will not resign.' She publicly wept and emerged as Kejriwal's choice to hoist the tricolour on Independence Day in his absence.

Mukesh Kumar said no one will assume charge of CM—'they would place his *khadau* (wooden slippers) on the throne and run the government.'

Few know that Atishi was born in a family of leftists. Her parents named her after two prominent Marxists—Marx and Lenin and she became Atishi Mar-Lena. Conscious of her surname, while BJP was targeting AAP leaders for pursuing soft Hindutva, she dropped her surname, Marlena.

Arvind Kejriwal was arrested on 21 March 2024, just ahead of the General Elections in the country. He was released on a twenty-one-day interim bail on 10 May 2024, during which time, he did hectic campaigning across the country.

Despite his fiery campaigning during this period of freedom from jail, AAP could win only three of the twenty-two Lok Sabha seats the party had contested. Delhi did not stand or sympathise with him as AAP lost all the four Lok Sabha seats it contested, but polled about twenty-five per cent votes. The Excise scam had dented Kejriwal and his party's image and it reflected in the 2025 Delhi poll results.

Historically, even when it has been in the best of health, AAP has not won a single seat in Delhi Lok Sabha polls. Delhi has always voted Kejriwal for CM and Narendra Modi for PM.

While returning to Tihar jail on the evening of 2 June 2024, Kejriwal had told his demoralised party workers that he was going back to jail 'not because he was involved in corruption, but because he had raised his voice against dictatorship,' as reported by the media. Despite several petitions, he continued to remain in jail on technical grounds and was finally released on bail on 12 September 2024.

AAP had pinned its hopes for its recovery from Haryana and Delhi Assembly Elections which were due in October 2024 and February 2025 respectively. AAP had launched the 'son of the soil campaign' in Haryana, but could not win any of the eighty-nine seats it had contested. The party polled barely 1.53 per cent votes.

Despite being a member of the I.N.D.I.A. Bloc, AAP had not allied with the Congress as Kejriwal wanted a solo show in the Delhi polls in February 2025. He ended roughing it out on Delhi streets fighting both the BJP and the Congress.

Kejriwal had quit the prestigious All India Revenue Services to fight corruption and had launched an energetic campaign to demand the Jan Lokpal Bill (Citizen Ombudsman Bill).

Kejriwal has also been an energetic RTI activist and earlier, ran an NGO called 'Parivartan.' Kejriwal as an RTI activist often sought information on inflated power bills, bungling in the construction of roads and visited newspaper offices to share the startling revelations that came in the form of answers. He even met journalists at selected places to show and share these documents.

A byproduct of an anti-corruption movement, Kejriwal has maintained a brave face though the fear of going back to jail must have been haunting him. His wife, Sunita Kejriwal has been confidently defending her husband, saying, 'If Arvind can be corrupt, then no one can be honest.' Power might have gone to his head, but did it corrupt him? The answer lies with the investigative authorities and the courts—legal and public.

However, AAP workers who always had a streak of activism in them, having organised massive protests even when the party was in power, were somewhat feeble in their several demonstrations in Delhi against these unpalatable developments, which many described as politics of vendetta.

They did not organise any public referendum on the arrest, harassment and humiliation of their leaders by the Narendra Modi government in the Delhi Excise Scam, though the party insists there was no scam, kickbacks or money trail.

In 2011, they had taken Delhi by storm on their demand

for the Lokpal Bill, holding public debates and discussions. In January 2014, Kejriwal as Delhi CM along with his senior ministers and leaders had defied police orders to stage a 10-day-long protest at Railway Bhawan, demanding action against police officers who had refused to carry out a raid in an alleged drug and prostitution racket. Kejriwal had then declared, 'They all say I am an anarchist. Yes, I am an anarchist.'

Why did AAP volunteers and supporters not go to the public like they had done before on public issues? Did they lack the spine or the backbone or had they weakened? The answer is simple. Who could have organised such a ground mobilisation in the absence of both Kejriwal and Sisodia?

Perhaps Kejriwal must be repenting now for not building a structured organisation, while spreading wings in the country! Observers say the party is in disarray in Delhi and losing ground in Punjab.

Is AAP in danger?

AAP, a new phenomenon in Indian politics, is in danger today, but the party will stay and survive till Arvind Kejriwal is around. He is the main target of attack. However, the pertinent question is how would AAP go down in the annals of Indian political history: As a party who fought corruption, but itself turned corrupt? Or, as a party who fought corruption in public life, corruption charges in personal life and emerged victorious?

Senior journalist Pankaj Vohra said, 'AAP's future is linked to Kejriwal's future. If he remains in jail, then the party is in trouble. He made a fundamental mistake in selecting Rajya Sabha members and has few friends. He should be able to discern between loyalists and seasonal friends.'

As of now, the top leadership of the AAP stands united, but

the BJP would like to weaken it, and break it. Kejriwal is still popular, but the party needs a well-oiled machinery for posterity. Sisodia may now fix the nuts and bolts, though he himself had to change his constituency during this election.

Why has AAP reached such a scary state?

Strangely, AAP which practised participatory politics and believed in the consultative character of the government, fell prey to the cult politics of mainline parties.

Kejriwal became the undisputed boss who often took decisions unilaterally, wilfully ignoring the advice of his colleagues or bureaucrats, so much so that a senior bureaucrat was reportedly manhandled by his people in front of him, leading the officer to walk out of the meeting. It had become the talk of the town.

Also, AAP does not have a clear second-rung leader. Manish Sisodia was second in command, whom the BJP sent to jail first, to break the party's backbone. But his future remains uncertain as he is out on bail, too.

Sanjay Singh played a key role in the distribution of tickets and in other decisions. He has been loyal to Kejriwal. Much would now depend on him as well as on Sunita Kejriwal. Even those who adore Kejriwal have a common grievance against him. They all say that 'He doesn't listen.'

Dissenting voices, which were once welcomed by him were silenced, and leaders purged irrespective of their status, contribution or value to the party.

Kejriwal had become so conscious about his image that he often sat right in the centre of a huge *dewan* at his home with his legs crossed like Gandhi, while meeting people, something that was noticed and discussed by most of his visitors.

While a section of leaders had suggested building a party

structure before entering national politics, Kejriwal had bulldozed their ideas and the rebels, too, soon fell in line.

AAP contested 432 of the 543 seats in the 2014 polls, despite the teething problems and skeleton presence in the country. Kejriwal also decided to challenge the BJP's prime ministerial candidate Narendra Modi in his stronghold of Varanasi. Obviously, he lost the elections, but emerged as a national figure, ending second in the race. Kejriwal smiled as AAP won four seats polling 2.1 per cent votes in its maiden Lok Sabha polls.

Five years later, in the 2019 Lok Sabha polls, the party's performance dipped as it won only one seat out of the thirty-five it contested. In 2024, when the party was in complete disarray, AAP contested twenty-two seats and won three. In the process, AAP's organisational structure moved from volunteer-based to paid workers, from crowd funding to corporate funding.

Yet, even in its poor health, AAP could mobilise a section of society, which is irreligious, progressive and is completely disenchanted by the political system that is ingrained in the caste or communal cesspool.

But can AAP retain its unique ubiquitous character in Delhi?

A senior party functionary describes as 'unfortunate,' the dilution of the distinct political values for which the party was earlier identified with.

'We worked hard in Punjab and built a volunteer-based campaign in 2017, which actually paid dividends in 2022. But today we have both, the paid volunteers and the natural volunteers and the groups often clash. Also, there are so many first-timers who need guidance—they lack political acumen. But who's there to guide them?' he says.

Kejriwal has not cultivated many friends in the opposition parties.

The importance of friends in a political ecosystem was realised by late UP Chief Minister Mulayam Singh Yadav quite late in the day. 'Almost all leaders in the Lok Sabha had come out in my support when FIRs were being lodged against me in police stations by the BSP,' he had said with pride. There was a time when Mulayam, also a wrestler, used to roll up his sleeves at the slightest provocation.

Few came in support of Kejriwal when he needed them the most. It is said that he is ruthlessly selfish in watching his or his party's interests. Interestingly, some of his senior leaders wanted AAP to enter into electoral alliances with like-minded parties till they were strong enough to fight battles on their own, but Kejriwal stood his ground against alliances and selectively picked his poll partners.

In 2024, Kejriwal relented and agreed to become a part of the Opposition bloc, I.N.D.I.A., but in Punjab, he refused to share seats with the Congress. It was the same in Delhi, where despite the heat from the BJP's quarters, both Kejriwal and Congress remained adamant on contesting independently.

His IITian batchmates are among his best friends, besides some journalists. In the world of politics, he maintains a rapport with Chandrababu Naidu, Mamata Banerjee, Akhilesh Yadav, Manish Tiwari and MK Stalin to name a few. But he trusts none.

He is very fond of his family; they are his strength. Every success and victory is celebrated with them with a hug to his wife and *charan sparsh* (touching feet in respect) of his parents.

'He is sharp and a focused guy, reads a lot, and will not allow anyone to operate his twitter (now X) handle for him. Stubbornness is both his strength and weakness. He is passionate about his mission and actually believes that what he thinks or decides is right,' said one of Kejriwal's associates.

His one quality that senior journalist Ashutosh had said to an anchor in a show, is his 'single-minded focus' which he describes as 'amazing'.

In 2024, AAP had a running government in Punjab and a paralysed government in the country's capital in Delhi when Delhi elections were announced.

A quote of Mahatma Gandhi, again from his website, mirrors the party's turbulent journey. 'First they ignore you, then they laugh at you, then they fight you and then you win.'

This is precisely what AAP leaders, dressed in casual T-shirts and trousers instead of archetypical white starched kurta-pyjama, have experienced. Only they could not sustain their wins for long.

Most of them are family men, whose spouses accompany them to political functions, but they do not hold positions.

AAP now faces an existential crisis

Sanjay Singh is hopeful as he says that 'we are fighters who never give up on our mission'.

> The party's fate is tied directly to Kejriwal. One has to remember that the party is barely eleven years old. AAP is a young party with young leaders. When an attack of this sort is made, the very foundations are tested. "This is the moment for AAP", a party leader told *Indian Express*.'(Mallica Joshi, Jatin Anand, Apurva Vishwanath on 22 March 2024)

Former minister in the AAP government, Saurabh Bhardwaj had told the media, 'Parties with core strength do not stop existing at a time of crisis. We have stood against the BJP tactics all these years and we would continue to do so. The party's obituary has been written countless times only to be erased.'

His supporters feel Kejriwal paid the price for his decision to challenge Narendra Modi in his maiden 2014 election from

Varanasi and the personal attacks on him. The BJP's humiliating defeat in the Delhi Assembly Elections in 2015, when it was reduced to three and Congress to a big zero could be the trigger. Author Pushparaj V Deshpande had written then:

> Aam Aadmi Party's victory in the recently concluded Delhi assembly elections is being hailed as a rejection of divisive politics. It has been argued that this result has 'protected the soul of India' and restored 'an equilibrium…in the national polity'. People have gone so far as to argue that the results have inflicted a "glorious humiliation on the BJP brass" and were a defeat of "BJP's Hindu's Delusions." This liberal triumphalism is however an oversimplification. AAP fought and won this election tactically. It scrupulously stuck to what has been characterised by Chief Minister Arvind Kejriwal himself as *kaam ki rajniti*.' (Excerpted from an article on the 'The Future of Progressive Politics in India.')

So far, what has worked for Kejriwal is that he has no ideology—neither rightist nor leftist; he neither promotes Hindutva, nor opposes it. He visits temples, takes a holy dip in the Ganga, launches a paid *teerth yatra* scheme and so on. He has often played by the ear and retained support of migrants, Sikhs, Muslims, Dalits and Vaish communities. His ideology is that of the common man as his speeches are bereft of caste and communal pampering.

I asked his one-time close associate on how Kejriwal spent his days in jail? What would he do first after his release?

The answer was: 'He is an angry man, revengeful, detached and sleeps less. He is a loner, planner and thinker. Today time is tougher than when Hazare had deserted them in September 2012. BJP wants to crush AAP. The excise scam has dented, but not demolished its image. But he is also a fighter.'

The first thing he will do is to take on Modi and Shah head on! He knows the leaders may leave, but the party volunteers would be back with him. He fought as a warrior in the battle ground and lost.

He has health issues and that's always a concern.

The party would survive. The first ever unique experiment in Indian politics will not fail as more Kejriwals will be born.

Chapter 11

Small Parties are Coalition Linchpins

From the revolutionary leader Netaji Subhash Chandra Bose, to social activists, film stars and set designers, all have founded regional parties, which dot the political landscape of the country.

Netaji founded the All India Forward Bloc (AIFB) in 1939 at Makur, Unnao, after resigning from the Congress party. The ageing party at 84 is still alive with a desire to revive itself, as it walks, in both letter and spirit, on Netaji's message of 'Victory and defeat are not important; the fight itself is everything.'

Largely active in pockets of West Bengal and Kerala, AIFB is afflicted with multiple health issues like a financial crunch and a sharp dip in the party's membership and vote share. The party has no MP or MLA and as an ally of an ailing Left Front, its revival appears near impossible. However, AIFB is going ahead with its rejuvenation campaign titled, 'We are Subhasist.' They also plan to enroll new members from their ongoing mass movements and agitations.

AIFB general secretary Debabrata Biswas is confident that Subhasism would show the country a way towards 'Justice, Equality, Democracy, Discipline, Love,' the five pillars of their amended preamble of the party's Constitution. 'Our presence is everywhere and we will take Subhasism everywhere,' is his confident refrain.

The Vikassheel Insaan Party (VIP) was created by a set designer in Bollywood, Mukesh Sahani, who projects himself as 'Son of Mallah' in the political world. He belongs to Bihar's Extremely Backward Caste (EBC).

His rag-to-riches story is like any Bollywood thriller—an 18-year-old who grew up in abject poverty leaves home in search of livelihood, migrates to the city of dreams, Mumbai, toils hard and makes it big in Bollywood, and then launches his event management company, returns home to find people living knee-deep in poverty and decides to work for their upliftment, especially Mallahas and Nishads.

Instead of joining any one of the established political parties, Mukesh decided to float his own party to serve his community better. He launched VIP in 2018.

Initially, Mukesh had associated with the BJP, but soon he switched over to the Mahagatbandhan. VIP won four seats in the 2020 Bihar Assembly polls and he became minister of state for animal husbandry, a post from which he was removed in 2022 after Chief Minister Nitish Kumar joined hands with the BJP. Three MLAs of the VIP also deserted him for power and protection. It's not the end of the story as yet as Mukesh has already allied with the RJD for the 2025 Assembly Polls and his party is likely to contest three seats.

Cut to the South, where film stars who are worshipped like demigods in some of the states have been successful. But they have failed, too, as after floating their party, they lacked the wherewithal to run their organisation.

Three popular Kollywood film stars—Rajinikant, Vijayakanth

and Kamal Haasan—had also founded their political outfits, which fizzled out after creating a hype.

The Desiya Murpokku Dravida Kazhagam (DMDK) was founded by popular film star Vijayakanth in 2005 and has fought elections, both solo as well as in alliance with the Left and with AIADMK, but power remained elusive till his death in 2023. He had then become leader of the opposition. Now his wife, Premalatha is the General Secretary of the party.

Makkal Needhi Maiam was founded by superstar Kamal Haasan in 2018. Despite the excitement he had created with his statement, 'No right, no left,' Haasan polled 2.62 per cent votes in the 2021 Assembly polls. He lost his seat too. Kamal Haasan's party is now on the wane.

Rajinikanth starred in 170 films, but his party could not take off. He announced plans to launch Rajini Makkal Mandram (RMM) in 2018, but dismantled it midway with his workers returning to Rajinikanth Fans Welfare Forum.

Now, the entry of another popular film star and playback singer Joseph Vijay, referred to by fans and media as Thalapathy (commander), has created quite a flutter in political circles. He has acted in about seventy films. He has floated the Tamilaga Vettri Kazhagam (TVK) in February 2024. The 2026 Assembly polls in Tamil Nadu will decide if he will last on the poll scene.

Interestingly, the founders of regional parties or even their families rarely wind up their outfits even after they have gone defunct. The ECI has listed about sixty defunct parties in the country, which need to be deleted from its pages for ever. The highest number of defunct parties are in Kerala, followed by Tamil Nadu and Punjab.

The small and tiny regional parties have been set up in different time frames, since the pre-Independence era till today, though there were phases when they mushroomed in the years 1967, 1977 and 1989, primarily to challenge the dominance of the Congress party.

These regional parties—tiny, small and big—are active, inactive, recognised or unrecognised. They have split and survived, flourished and fizzled, died and disappeared, but their political space and sway has not shrunk. The numbers may have marginally changed.

Some of these regional parties are tiny, but, they still dictate and dominate the national parties as well as the bigger regional parties, as they have captive votes of their caste or community, sometimes in some pockets only. But they wield immense bargaining power in closely contested elections and in hung houses. They refuse mergers to maintain their independent identity, as in the choppy waters of politics, the big fish often eats up the small fish.

Academically though, there are many answers to why these tiny parties are thriving. One cogent reason is the abject failure of the two major national parties—the Congress and the BJP—to develop local leadership, which aligns and affirms local issues of culture, caste and communities in the states, notably the Southern-Western region.

The Central leadership of the national parties have marginalised these leaders instead of grooming leadership among castes and communities. Maybe after Indira Gandhi became a mass leader who could win elections across the country, the party decided to clip their wings. The BJP, despite a mass leader in Narendra Modi are using smaller parties in elections rather than developing leadership in the party.

The other reason why smaller parties are thriving could be because of splits in political parties, with the splinter groups adding to the list of regional parties, and sometimes going defunct. Three sets of examples can be cited.

The Suheldev Bharatiya Samaj Party (SBSP) of Om Prakash Rajbhar in Uttar Pradesh is one such example. His strength is the Rajbhar votes in some pockets of East UP. It is still not a recognised state party, but demands national visibility. Rajbhar who changes partners and still remains in demand, says '*mein akela sab par bhari*,' (I alone can take on all) as he shakes hands with the Union Home Minister Amit Shah who persuades or pushes the Chief Minister Yogi Adityanath to take him into his cabinet, ignoring the abuses he had hurled at the CM some months back. The BJP and the SP will need an equally vocal Rajbhar leader to counter him.

Another example is the All India Indira Congress (Tiwari), which figures in the list of defunct parties. It was formed by three Congress stalwarts-turned-rebels, Narayan Datt Tiwari, Arjun Singh, Natwar Singh and others in 1996, protesting against the elevation of Narasimha Rao as PM and of Sita Ram Kesari as the first non-Brahmin President of the Congress. The party fought a couple of elections, but couldn't poll more than 1 per cent vote. It later merged with the Congress.

> **Caste Groups:** Kerala Congress was founded in 1964 and split two ways in 1979. One of the splinter group Kerala (M) has influence among the Christian voters, that too in the region of Travancore. It has one MP each in both the houses of Parliament and is a part of the ruling Left alliance after winning five seats in the 2021 Polls. Another splinter group Kerala Congress (Joseph) is active in central Kerala and enjoys the support of Syrian Christians and the Nair community. It has two seats in the State Assembly. Kerala Congress still exists.
>
> (*Indian Express*, 7 June 2024)

Ironically, even the big regional parties have not groomed leadership among castes and communities like Kanshi Ram at the district level.

The founder-President of the Samajwadi Party in Uttar Pradesh, Mulayam Singh Yadav had consistently projected and promoted leaders of different castes and sub-castes. While people remember only Amar Singh and Azam Khan as his buddies, Mulayam had many political stalwarts as his friends like Janeshwar Mishra, Mohan Singh, Ramsaran, SPS Baghel, Ram Govind Chaudhary, Ahmad Hasan and Beni Prasad Verma, as he truly believed in his ideologue Ram Manohar Lohia's words that caste would remain an integral ingredient of Indian society and elections, and therefore, it should be given due representation.

His son and SP national president Akhilesh Yadav's much-touted PDA (*Pichra, Dalit* and *Alpasankhyak*) formula is straight from his father's book. It delivered him huge gains in the 2024 General Elections. By winning thirty-seven seats, it is today the third largest party in the eighteenth Lok Sabha.

Over the years, the lower castes and their sub castes, aware of their political rights, are asserting themselves, demanding a share in power. In their urge for economic and social empowerment, they support tiny parties led by their caste leaders, who at the time of elections bargain and blackmail bigger parties.

Some of them are also born out of movements for smaller states, tribal rights and empowerment of castes and communities.

The late 1980s saw an end of Brahmin hegemony and the beginning of backward caste politics in the country. Vishwanath Pratap Singh, a Rajput leader in the Congress saw an opportunity in the OBC's demand for empowerment. He promised implementation of the Mandal Commission report that recommended 27 per cent reservation for OBCs.

Singh was Union Defence Minister in the Congress government at the Centre and had launched a campaign to tarnish the image of then Prime Minister Rajiv Gandhi by publicly raising the controversial issue of Bofors kickbacks. He was sacked.

Singh had formed the Jan Morcha in 1987, which he merged with the Janata Party, Lok Dal, and Indian National Congress to form the Janata Dal in October 1988 and and the National Front to form the government after the 1989 General Elections. Congress emerged as the single largest party, but declined to form the government. The President invited Janata Dal, the second largest group, supported by the BJP and the Communists to keep their enemy number one, the Congress out of power.

The rest is history. The country saw seven Prime Ministers and five elections between 1989 and 1999, which included a five-year rule of the Congress government led by Prime Minister PV Narasimha Rao from 1991-1996.

Taking a dig at the Prime Minister IK Gujral, heading the United Front government from April 1997 to March 1998, Sushma Swaraj had said in Parliament, 'I don't know why you have accepted this position. You are like a bride/daughter-in-law in a joint family with several warring in-laws and she is expected to appease all.' Incidentally, he was the consensus candidate though the Yadav chieftains, Lalu Yadav and Mulayam Singh Yadav, were also claimants for the Prime Minister's post.

What happened to the Janata Dal? The formidable leaders split and formed their political outfits in their own pocket boroughs across the country-Samata Party, JD(S), BJD, Rashtriya Lok Morcha, JD(U), RJD, Samajwadi Party, Loktantrik Janata Dal, Indian National Lok Dal, Lok Janshakti Party, *et al.* At least five splinter groups of the Janata Dal figure in the defunct list.

The original Janata Dal was dissolved in 2003.

The late BJP CM Kalyan Singh often used to sing a parody, '*Janata Dal ke Tukde Hazar Huye, kuch Idhar Gire, Kuch Udhar Gire,*' which was partly true as ego-clashes did not allow the regional satraps to stay together for long.

However, the Ram temple hero of the BJP had failed to comprehend the challenges that these splinter groups would then throw to the BJP in several states in the years to come.

The backward castes, the backbone of the Janata Dal, have also continued to hold veto power till date and their first choice has been non-Congress and non-BJP parties. Most of these political parties have been flourishing in their respective states, stopping the BJP in their tracks in several states, till the Modi magic started working.

VP Singh revived the Jan Morcha sometime in 2005 with cine star and politician Raj Babbar becoming its public face, but he later joined the Congress after failing to even get noticed in the 2007 UP Assembly Polls. VP Singh's son Ajeya Pratap Singh also tried to infuse life in the dying Jan Morcha before the 2009 General Elections. He had also contested elections from Fatehpur only to lose it. He merged the party with the Congress and quit active politics.

Janata Dal was a national party, but it was a coalition of smaller parties and they all took the independent route.

Jat leader from Haryana and two-time deputy Prime Minister in the Janata Dal government (1989-90, 1990-1991) Chaudhary Devi Lal had formed Indian National Lok Dal (INLD) in 1996 and passed the baton of Haryana's first regional party to his son, Om Prakash Chautala in 1999. Devi Lal died in 2001. INLD remained a member of NDA and had secured four and five Lok Sabha seats in the 1998 and 1999 General Elections.

Chautala became CM in 1999 with BJP support and again

in 2000, but his 5 years and 224-day long tenure was plagued by corruption and he was convicted in 2013. He was released only in 2021.

Family feuds are obvious in family-controlled parties. The internecine troubles had erupted in Devi Lal's family in 2018 over the control of the INLD. It split a successful regional party and culminated in its complete downfall within six years.

Devi Lal's grandson Abhay Singh headed INLD against which his great grandsons, Dushyant and Digvijay Singh had formed the Jannayak Janta Party (JJP). The warring factions faced electoral highs and lows with their vote share falling to 1.48 per cent (INLD) and 0.87 per cent (JJP) in the 2024 General Elections.

The family of the tallest leader of the state went around seeking votes to save their party symbols in the subsequent Assembly polls. Eight family members contested, but only two won the polls. Former deputy CM Dushyant Chautala (JJP) ended fifth in the race on his seat, losing his deposit.

Is it the end of the Devi Lal era or of INLD and JJP as the state went bi-polar in the subsequent Assembly polls in 2024? Experts like Ramesh Vinayak said both the regional parties are staring at an existential crisis after their crushing defeat in the 2024 Assembly elections, but it may still be too early to write their obituaries.

***

There were six national parties, fifty-seven state recognised parties and 2,764 unrecognised parties in the country in 2024. The national parties are: BJP, Congress, BSP, AAP, CPI(M) and National People's Party (NPP).

The majority of the recognised regional parties had come

under a larger umbrella, the BJP-led National Democratic Alliance and the Congress-led United Progressive Alliance, rechristened as I.N.D.I.A. There are very few parties that operate independently.

This is why

From 1989 to 1999, the country was ruled by seven Prime Ministers. VP Singh (Janata Dal), and Chandrashekhar (Samajwadi Janata Party) lasted from December 1989 to June 1991. Congress Prime Minister Narasimha Rao completed his tenure from 1991 to 1996.

Thereafter, the BJP had emerged as the single largest party in 1996. The President, Shankar Dayal Sharma invited the party leader Atal Bihari Vajpayee to form the government. The government fell in thirteen days. Subsequently, the United Front government was formed by state level regional parties, supported by the Congress. HD Deve Gowda ruled for 324 days and Inder Kumar Gujral for 332 days. Mid-term elections were held.

Again, after the 1998 Lok Sabha polls, Vajpayee formed the Central Government, which, however, collapsed after thirteen months when he lost the trust vote by a single vote. The country had to bear the brunt of five mid-term polls between 1989 and 1999.

The unpalatable developments propelled Atal Bihari Vajpayee to form the National Democratic Alliance with like-minded regional parties, which had contested the 1999 elections and completed their full term. The Congress also constituted the United Progressive Alliance which had won the 2004 and 2009 Lok Sabha elections with late Congress Prime Minister Manmohan Singh ruling the country for a decade.

As the relevance of the regional parties grew in national politics, their voice also became louder. They stayed with their respective conglomerates as it gave small parties a collective strength. Even the BJP high command did not dismantle the NDA though the party became self-reliant in the 2014 and 2019 Lok Sabha polls.

Not only had the members of the NDA bailed out Prime Minister Narendra Modi from a crisis, but two regional parties had come forward to help him accomplish his dream of a consecutive third term. On its own, the BJP had won 240 seats in a house of 543 in the 2024 Lok Sabha polls.

With over two-dozen poll partners, spread across the country, the BJP had entered the electoral fray with a target of 400 plus. Only a dozen of these poll partners had contributed about twenty-five seats (the larger share came from the breakaway group of Shiv Sena), compelling the PM to borrow support from TDP and JD(U).

About 20-odd members of NDA had not contested the elections and thus have no representation in Parliament. But they had mustered support of their castes and communities for BJP nominees like the Suheldev Bhartiya Samaj Party of Om Prakash Rajbhar, who after flip flops, had joined the NDA months before the 2024 polls. He was awarded a berth in the Uttar Pradesh cabinet.

Overnight, the government converted from a BJP-led coalition government to an NDA government.

In Tamil Nadu, where the BJP has not yet cultivated its support base, it has tied up with smaller parties like the Pattali Makkal Katchi (PMK), founded by S Ramadoss, a Rajya Sabha member. He has been a member of the NDA since 2014. The party's influence is limited to the Vanniyar caste in Northern Tamil Nadu.

TMC (Moopanar) is a breakaway faction of the Congress that was formed in 1996, and Amma Makkal Munnetra Kazhagam

(AMMK) formed in 2018, has a support base of about 0.8 to 2.5 per cent votes. The tie-up with small parties jacked up BJP's vote share from 3.5 per cent in 2019 to 11 per cent in 2024 in the southern state.

The 72-member Council of Ministers headed by Narendra Modi was sworn in on 8 June 2024 in which both the pre- and post-poll allies were awarded thirty-six berths.

Even tiny parties share power at the Centre, while others like Nishad Party and Suheldev Bhartiya Samaj Party (SBSP) were rewarded with ministerial berths in the Yogi Adityanath government in Uttar Pradesh.

Both are unrecognised state parties, the third category mentioned by the ECI on its website besides the defunct ones.

The beneficiaries in the Central Government include Apna Dal and Rashtriya Lok Dal from UP, Shiv Sena, RPI from Maharashtra, JD(U), LJP and Hindustan Awami Morcha from Bihar, JD(S) from Karnataka, TDP, Andhra Pradesh, to mention a few.

Apna Dal (AD), has been a constant ally of the BJP since the 2014 Lok Sabha polls. The regional party with pockets of influence in East UP, including Narendra Modi's Lok Sabha constituency of Varanasi, had won one Lok Sabha seat in the elections.

AD was formed by Kurmi leader, Sonelal Patel in 1995 to build an alliance of the Kurmi-Muslims on the lines of Dalit-Muslims of BSP and Yadav-Muslims of Samajwadi Party.

Patel, who was considered close to Kanshi Ram, had quit the BSP in 1995 after holding a convention of Kurmi leaders, cutting across party lines in Lucknow, to demand better representation for them, both in politics and administration. Kurmis are the second largest backward caste in the state.

He was general secretary of the BSP and president of UP Kurmi Mahasabha.

A postgraduate in science and law, he had brazenly declared his political mission as secular, and of politically empowering all communities minus Thakurs and Brahmins. Kurmis contribute funds to the party, a model he had picked from the BSP.

Patel had first hit the headlines after his Muslim candidate had won from Brahmin Rajput-dominated Pratapgarh constituency in central UP.

While Sonelal Patel wanted to unite the Kurmis of the state, his own family split into two factions. Apna Dal (Kamerawadi) is led by his wife Krishna Patel. His daughter, Pallavi Patel who chose to side with her mother, later won the State Assembly elections on a Samajwadi Party ticket in 2022. The other faction, AD (Sonelal) was formed by his other daughter, Union minister Anupriya Patel.

The family were divided over claims on the Rohaniya assembly seat, which Anupriya had vacated after her election to the Lok Sabha in 2014. Both her mother and her husband had staked their claim on the seat.

Anupriya, who has been minister in the Modi government since 2014 had formed AD(S) in 2016, which was also recognised by the Election Commission of India. The dispute is pending in the court while the family keeps washing its dirty linen in public.

As for its electoral performance in the assembly polls, AD(S) had won one seat (0.90 per cent votes) in 2012, nine seats (0.98 per cent votes) in 2017 and twelve seats (1.6 per cent votes) in 2022.

In the Lok Sabha polls, AD(S) had won two seats each in 2014 and 2019, and one seat in 2024, polling between 0.92 per cent to 1.21 per cent votes.

Recently in an interview to *Indian Express*, while answering a question on change in BJP's approach in 2024 after it lost the brute majority it had in 2014 and 2019, Anupriya had said, 'We are seeing change in the way the PM talks. He doesn't talk about the BJP but NDA.'

The other major gainer is Rashtriya Lok Dal (RLD) founded by political stalwart Chaudhary Ajit Singh in 1996 after parting ways with the Janata Dal.

It originated from the Lok Dal, which his father and former Prime Minister Charan Singh had formed in 1979, merging Janata Party, Socialist Party and Janata Dal(S). It had suffered several splits, the last one in 1987 when two factions, Lok Dal (A) and Lok Dal (B) emerged from it. The first was led by his foreign-returned son, Chaudhary Ajit Singh while the Mulayam Singh Yadav-led Lok Dal (B) also staked claim on his legacy. Ajit Singh eventually formed Rashtriya Lok Dal in 1996, a breakaway faction of the Janata Dal. His son, Jayant Chaudhary heads it, now.

As a small regional party, RLD had gone through several highs and lows, but its leader Chaudhary Ajit Singh managed to retain hold on pockets of West UP and a berth in the Union Cabinet, irrespective of who headed it—Congress, BJP or United Front. However, his party base kept shrinking as they could not follow Charan Singh's much acclaimed formula of AJGR (rainbow coalition of Ahir, Jat, Gujar, Rajputs to which he later added Muslims).

Ahead of the 2024 General Elections, Jayant Chaudhary was lured into the NDA bloc by the Union Government's gracious announcement of the Bharat Ratna for his grandfather Charan Singh. This was the long pending demand of the Jats whom the government wanted to mollify.

Jayant snapped ties with the Samajwadi Party and contested two Lok Sabha seats in alliance with the BJP. He won both the seats, polling 0.14 per cent votes.

In a first ever, he is now a minister in the Modi government and is judiciously pursuing issues of region and not religion in politics. He also has plans to expand the party base in East UP.

RLD has nine seats in the UP State Assembly and a minister in the Yogi government.

While sharing the dais with Akhilesh Yadav (SP), Jayant had said, '*mein chavani nahi hun jo flip karoonga* (I am not a 25 paise coin who will flip).' His quote had become the flavour of the election, as he had soon flipped and joined the BJP. People said it runs in his blood as his father used to frequently change partners.

Despite its limited presence in West UP, RLD is here to stay and will remain relevant as long as Jats continue to support the grandson of Charan Singh.

Lok Janshakti Party was founded by Ram Vilas Paswan in 2000 after parting ways from Janata Dal. The party had split between his brother Pashupati and son Chirag Paswan after his death in 2020.

Chirag, who has worked in Bollywood, had formed a breakaway faction LJP(RV) in 2021 and become a member of NDA. Now with a hundred per cent strike rate in the General Elections, in which he won all five seats, Chirag like Jayant Chaudhary is enjoying his maiden stint in Yogi 3.0. He is the Dalit face that BJP would want to exploit in the 2025 Bihar State Assembly Polls.

Hindustani Awam Morcha(S), founded by Jitan Ram Manjhi in Bihar in 2015 after he had separated from JD(U) leader and CM Nitish Kumar is a minister of state in the Modi government. He had won his maiden Lok Sabha election in 2024 and is an ally of NDA.

Why would these tiny parties quit NDA, when they can enjoy power as ministers, while being an ally at the Centre or in their respective regions?

Have you heard of parties like Indigenous People's Front of Tripura (IPFT)—Tipra Motha Party, Bharat Dharma Jana Sena—Kerala, Jan Surajya Shakti (Maharashtra), and the Prahar Janshakti Party?

The opposition bloc I.N.D.I.A. initially had twenty-six members at the time of its creation. It eventually allied with thirty-seven parties in the 2024 Lok Sabha elections. The Congress won ninety-nine seats, the regional parties won the remaining 139, the major chunk coming from SP, DMK, Shiv Sena (UBT), NCP(SP), AAP and RJD.

Though the formation of I.N.D.I.A. was aimed at forcing a direct contest between the joint opposition candidates and the BJP nominees, the plan was derailed because of conflict of interest in some states like West Bengal, Kerala and Punjab.

It was not a problem of plenty, but clash of interests or egos as some of the regional parties have grown by grabbing the traditional votes of the Congress and thus would not want the grand old party to revive in their respective states.

For instance, while the Samajwadi Party would want to ally with the Congress and even support formation of its government at the Centre, it would not at any cost yield space to its one-time *bete noire*. Similar is the story of RJD in Bihar. The TMC and NCP are a breakaway faction of the Congress.

Now new parties are surfacing in Bihar, Tamil Nadu and UP.

Azad Samaj Party (Kanshi Ram) founder president Chandrashekhar Azad (39) walked to the Lok Sabha as a prominent Dalit face from UP, after winning his maiden election in 2024 at a time when the BSP has no representative in Parliament. He contested as an independent, but after his win in the elections, his political stock has gone up.

Prashant Kishor, a successful poll strategist, who had shot

into fame after the victory of Nitish Kumar, Mamata Banerjee and Chandrababu Naidu, is now out to use his political skills for himself. He has been on a *padyatra* in his home state of Bihar for over a year, determined not to ally with any political party before or after the 2025 Assembly Elections. He floated Jan Suraaj in 2024.

The entry of a Brahmin will make the contest interesting in the backward-dominated politics of Bihar, which has not seen a Brahmin chief minister since the mid-1980s.

Apparently, the number of national parties have by and large remained static. This means either the regional parties are not making a bid outside their fiefdoms or have not been acceptable outside their territory.

The regional parties had become shareholders in the states, but had lacked an ideological base needed for the longevity of the alliances. We have seen two more formations in 1977 and 1989 in the form of Janata Party and Janata Dal.

Earlier, there were eight national parties and sixteen regional parties. Now the regional parties have grown to fifty-seven, while national parties have come down to six. Of the six national parties, the CPI(M), CPI, NCP and BSP can anytime lose their status of a national party, if they fail to improve their performance in the elections.

Questions are being raised about 'unethical' switchovers by smaller parties. A research paper had this to say:

> The proliferation of parties, however undemocratic it may sound, must be stopped. How many parties are needed for successful working of democracy is a debatable issue. But there does not appear to be any reason to have many fragmented small parties, particularly those with no well-defined ideological positions, and not a ghost's chance of coming to

> power and run a government. (Manoj Kumar, BSF, Researcher CPCS, Jaipur, in a research paper on 'Coalition Politics in India: History and Analysis of Political Alliances')

The aspirational voters, however, demand welfare along with self-pride or else they move away for populist deliveries like we saw in Maharashtra and Jharkhand in the 2024 polls in which schemes to financially empower women paid enough dividends to cut through anti-incumbency against the incumbent government.

However, the parties will have to be in power to convince the voters about instant delivery of benefits as promises may appeal to them, but not enough to fetch their votes. The incapacitated Aam Admi Party faced this dilemma in the Delhi polls.

The wins in West Bengal and Jharkhand, amid controversy over manipulation of Electronic Voting Machines, also somehow prove that regional parties in power manage elections better than in the opposition.

Epilogue

There is ample evidence of inter-dependence of national and regional parties in Indian politics, which becomes magnified when national parties fail to muster enough strength to stand on their own.

So, while political scientists have been sceptical about the longevity of regional parties, the latter have been reviving, surviving and thriving as voters recognise their role and relevance in a parliamentary democracy. Indian voters have surprised both pollsters and political parties by their choices and wisdom.

A fresh challenge has now come from the BJP's decision to push One Nation, One Election (ONOE) in the country. Parliament had passed in December 2024, The Constitution (129th Amendment) Bill, popularly known as the One Nation, One Election Bill. The Bill proposes amendments to enable simultaneous elections for the Lok Sabha and State Legislative Assemblies.

The concerns of the regional parties were addressed by the high-level committee, which had recommended ONOE to the Union Cabinet after elaborate consultations with stakeholders including forty-seven political parties. The committee had observed in its report, 'Holding simultaneous elections does not undermine the role of regional parties. In fact, it encourages a more localised focus during elections, enabling regional parties to highlight the unique concerns and aspirations. This setup fosters a political environment where local issues are not overshadowed by national election campaigns, thus preserving the relevance of the regional voices.'

But fears and concerns are floating in the air. Would simultaneous elections to the state assembly and the Lok Sabha marginalise regional parties and eclipse local issues?

The SP leadership has raised worries about a big mismatch between the resources, infra and electoral strategies of the state and national parties, diluting regional issues and impeding fair polls. Already, an atmosphere of mistrust prevails with the opposition parties led by the Congress repeatedly raising the issue of EVM manipulations.

Shyamlal Yadav, Senior Associate Editor in *Indian Express* has deep understanding of Indian politics. He explains lucidly: 'Regional parties have long played a crucial role in championing local issues, preserving socio-cultural identities, and representing marginalised communities often overlooked by national parties. The implementation of ONOE could potentially weaken these parties by shifting focus from local concerns to national narratives much like the pre-1967 era when national discourse dominated the political landscape. In states where voters tend to support national parties in Lok Sabha elections but prefer regional parties in state elections, ONOE may disrupt this split-voting pattern, diminishing the influence of regional forces. The regional parties are likely to face significant challenges but the dominance of any single national party is unlikely to be permanent.'

Actually, if we look at states like West Bengal, Tamil Nadu,

Bihar and Uttar Pradesh, regional parties are throwing the main challenge to the BJP, as the Congress has not as yet shown any signs of recuperation. The scenario is unlikely to change even if simultaneous elections were held in these states. SP, the third largest party in the Lok Sabha, is a one-state regional force, but is giving nightmares to the BJP in the critically important state of UP.

Also, the inter-dependence of the national and regional parties would persist for power and positions. Most of the regional parties have found their anchor in the BJP-led NDA or Congress-led I.N.D.I.A. This dependence is likely to continue.

Shyam Lal Yadav adds: 'To remain competitive, regional parties may need to adapt by redefining their roles and revising strategies. In a nation as pluralistic as ours, no single national party can be truly all-encompassing. As the aspirations of various communities continue to evolve, there will always be space for regional parties and with it, the emergence of new parties, leaders, and alliances.'

Former Chief Election Commissioner SY Qureshi observes, 'If the whole idea behind the ONOE is to impede the growth of the regional parties, then it's short-term. The regional parties would bounce back. They have not as yet put up a big fight for political exigencies as many of them were subjected to standard blackmail and arm twisting.'

Would they merge with national parties under pressure?

In an interview with *Indian Express*, Sharad Pawar had hinted at the merger of regional parties with national parties. I doubt this would happen as a merger deprives them of the power they wield as an independent entity—big or small—and this underscores why there have been more splits than reunions in recent years.

It needs to be emphasised that regional parties are here to stay. Internecine troubles are worrying them as the national parties are fishing in their troubled waters. It's all part of the political power play. Few setbacks would not kill regional parties. Coalitions may die but parties won't.

Eventually their numbers in the state assemblies and the Lok Sabha would decide if they will dictate, dominate or destabilise governments.

Continue watching the regional parties, perched on a see-saw, playing the game of thrones and taking on the role of kingmakers!

Acknowledgements

A friend, who lives day and night with books (he runs the oldest bookshop in Lucknow), said the other day, 'Who is reading politics? Write on a more exciting subject!'

To salvage my enthusiasm, I said: 'Of course, people are passionate about politics. If you are referring to the new generation, I find them quite inquisitive about how and why political parties win elections.'

In my forty-year-long innings as a journalist—from a reporter, graduating to editor of a national daily in Uttar Pradesh—politics has been my staple diet. The more volatile, the more thrilling was the experience.

Watching the country's politics from Lucknow—from where the road of power travels to Delhi—and reporting on the changing dynamics of the regional and national parties, has always been exciting. There was never a dull moment, especially when regional parties started dictating national parties. It was really mind-boggling to see their moves on the chessboard from close quarters, especially the maverick Mulayam and manipulative Kanshi Ram.

All this inspired me to write my fourth book on a matter that was so lively and full of unpredictable twists and turns—almost like a suspense movie plot or a thriller book serial.

I wish to personally thank each one of those who supported me and saw me through this book, took my calls, read my mails, answered my queries and allowed me to quote them.

I am also thankful to the Internet as research has become much easier than what it used to be.

How can I forget my colleagues at *Hindustan Times* and the newspaper's rich library! A big thank you to the people at the newspaper and the sacred library.

My special thanks to Renu Kaul Verma of Vitasta Publishing and her competent colleagues.

Last but not the least, a special word of gratitude to my family—Neha, Monaal and Vatsala—who always gave precedence to my passion for writing over their own dreams. Their critical appreciation was accepted with a grin, as it helped me to improve the script. My gratitude to my husband, Kanchan Kumar Aron, who continues to encourage me from the world he lives in. I would not have been an author had he not given me the confidence to pen my first book. And now the fourth.